Freestyle Machine Embroidery

Techniques and Inspiration for Fiber Art

Carol Shinn

INTERWEAVE.
interweavestore.com

Cover and Interior Design Mark Lewis
Editor Ann Budd
Technical Editor Tom Lundberg
Illustration Carol Shinn
Production Katherine Jackson
Photography Carol Shinn except where noted and the following, taken by Ann Swanson: pages 16, 17, 19, 34, 35, 36, 38, 47, 50, 51 (bottom), 74, 75, 76, 77, 80, 81 (bottom), 82, 84, 85, 92 (bottom), 86, 87, 88, 93, 96 (top), 97, 100, 101, 104 (top right, bottom right), 109, 110, 111, 117 (bottom left), 125, 128, 131, 132, 133.

Interweave Press LLC
201 East Fourth Street
Loveland, CO 80537-5655 USA
interweavestore.com

Printed in China by Asia Pacific Offset.

Library of Congress Cataloging-in-Publication Data

Shinn, Carol, 1948-
  Freestyle machine embroidery : techniques and inspiration for fiber art / Carol Shinn, author.
    p. cm.
  Includes bibliographical references and index.
  ISBN 978-1-59668-042-5 (pbk.)
  1. Embroidery, Machine. 2. Textile crafts. I. Title.
  TT772.S545 2009
  746.44--dc22

                              2008055299

10 9 8 7 6 5 4 3 2 1

My special thanks to...

Tom Lundberg, who encouraged me to send a book proposal to Interweave in the first place, and who then carefully edited my text, kept me on track, and made sure that what I wrote was clear.

My husband, Randall Shinn, who encouraged and supported this project, and who did a fabulous job with the photography and helped with much-needed technical support.

Barbara Lee Smith, who helped me make connections with other artists and helped me rethink the organization of the book.

Jane Sauer, who also helped me connect with other artists.

Tricia Waddell, the editorial director of books at Interweave, who made the process so easy.

Ann Budd, who edited the book one last time and helped me through each stage of the publishing process.

Kerry Jackson, who worked hard on all the images, sometimes making nearly impossible photo and diagram files into clear and beautiful examples.

Ann Swanson, who photographed many of the examples.

And to each of the wonderful artists in the book and to the collectors of their works who gave permission for the pieces to be included in this book.

Contents

Post No Bills, **Jane Kenyon 2007,
40" x 28" (101 x 71 cm). Thread
on water-soluble stabilizer. Photographer: Kenji Nagai. Courtesy
of the Jane Sauer Gallery.**

Introduction

I knew by the third grade that I wanted to be an artist, but it wasn't until the early 1970s that I found my greatest interest to be in the fiber arts. For fifteen years, I wove clothing, wall hangings, and tapestries. During the late 1980s, in graduate school at Arizona State University, I began to freestyle embroider with the sewing machine. Right from the beginning I was interested in the effects of mixing color with thread and creating a solidly stitched fabric surface. I am sure that this was the result of having spent years mixing colors of yarn at the loom. My first solidly stitched freestyle machine embroidery was Scenario #1, which took its inspiration from a collage made of magazine paper scraps.

Machine sewing was not part of the graduate curriculum, but I nonetheless was encouraged to continue with machine embroidery. I made a series of pieces about an imaginary life form, which I named *Speedworms* (see *Identifying the Species* on page 29 and *Veloxvermis sulphurostris* on page 44). I had no instruction in machine embroidery, and I spent many frustrating hours figuring out the "whys" of my mistakes and what seemed like the refusal of my machine to cooperate. When—through my

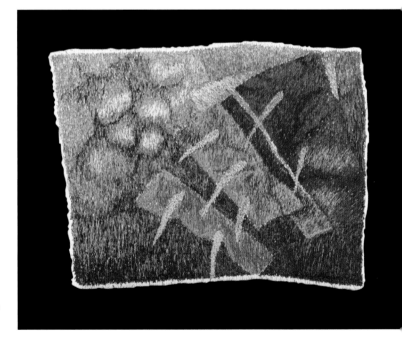

Opposite: *Curtain*, Carol Shinn 2005, 20" x 16¼" (51 x 42 cm). Machine stitching on fabric. Photographer: Carol Shinn. Collection of Susan Cargill, Birchwood, Wisconsin.

Scenario #1, Carol Shinn 1988, 9¾" x 13¼" (25 x 34 cm). Machine stitching on fabric. Photographer: Carol Shinn. Private collection.

own ignorance—I burned out the motor, my local sewing-machine dealer gave me a few lessons that greatly enhanced my understanding of the machine and the technique to which I had dedicated myself. The more I worked, the more problems resolved themselves. As I became more known for my work, I met other machine embroiderers around the country and learned tremendously from them and their work.

My artwork progressed as I continued to stitch. I mostly worked with one subject at a time in order to explore a particular subject and its related design problems. My work shifted from speedworms and the imaginary places they inhabited to scenes of desert landscapes. *Treeless Places #2* was one of several pieces set up to study the relative visual weight of different areas of a composition. Soon I was putting highways and cars in my landscapes

Treeless Places #2, Carol Shinn 1990, 22" x 20" (56 x 51 cm). Machine stitching on fabric. Photographer: Carol Shinn. Private collection.

Pink Shirt #1, Carol Shinn 1996, 14¾" x 16¼"
(38 x 42 cm). Machine stitching on fabric.
Photographer: Carol Shinn. Private collection.

(see *Exit 242* on page 27). By the mid-1990s, I was working with images from the parking lot of my neighborhood shopping center (*Pink Shirt #1*). I was interested in the design problems of connecting lines within a composition and framing information on the picture plane.

When I tired of new cars, I sought out old ones. In 2000, my husband and I spent the year in Las Cruces, New Mexico. A nearby car salvage yard allowed me the freedom to photograph as much as I wanted. I started a series using old cars as characters from Greek mythology. By then I had stopped using collaged imagery and was doing part of my designing with Photoshop on a desktop computer. My intent was to illustrate a particular pivotal moment in a story. In *Icarus Fallen* (see page 10), I equated the rippling desert sand to water and the partially buried car to Icarus.

Icarus Fallen, Carol Shinn 2001, 13¼" x 21½" (34 x 55 cm). Machine stitching on fabric. Photographer: Carol Shinn. Collection of Stephen and Linda Waterhouse.

Now, eight years later, I am stitching two bodies of work: one series studies how doors and windows isolate or frame information and the other features chairs that evoke the passage of time. Both series are about the moods of places and the beauty of tactile surfaces. As I look back on the works I have embroidered, I think they have always been about tactile surfaces.

Making my work is a solitary occupation. I balance that with teaching, which has enhanced my knowledge in several ways. By explaining my technique to others, I have learned to articulate what I do intuitively on my own, which in turn has helped my process develop further. Stitching samples for teaching presents me with more possibilities. In ad-dition, my students make discoveries along the way that add to my body of knowledge and sometimes change the way I work.

I wrote this book to share what I have learned over the past two decades. In the process of writing it down, new revelations have occurred, which I have incorporated. What I share here is only part of what is now possible with freestyle machine embroidery. Future changes will develop the field further. Freestyle machine embroidery—like drawing, painting, or any other of form of art making—is simply a technique waiting to be used. It is part of a dialogue between hands and mind. It is a form of communication. Connectedness and excitement grow as more artists contribute to the field. Join me on this path of discovery.

Flowered Upholstery, Carol Shinn 2007, 17½" x 12"
(45 x 31 cm). Machine stitching on fabric. Photographer:
Carol Shinn. Courtesy of the Hibberd McGrath Gallery.

Detail of *Curtain*, Carol Shinn 2005.

Chapter One:
Understanding the Process of Freestyle Machine Embroidery

Creative works—even the most radical—are the result of ordinary thinking processes.

–Robert Weisberg, author of *Creativity: Beyond the Myth of Genius*

What do we mean when we say "freestyle" machine embroidery? Embroidery has been created with sewing machines almost since they were invented. As decorative stitch settings were added to machines, ways of using them evolved. For years, the term machine embroidery included machine-controlled decorative stitches as well as freehand drawing with lines stitched by the machine.

Many new sewing machines have computer components for designing embroidery; the technology is fascinating. With the right software, you can translate a photograph or drawing into a design file, which the machine then translates into stitch lines and blocks of color. The result is a computerized interpretation of your idea; nonetheless, depending on your artistic experience and skill with the equipment, the result can be quite sensitive and beautiful. When the term machine embroidery is now used, it refers to this computerized process.

Since the advent of computerized machines, new terms and definitions have evolved to describe creative machine work that does not use embroidery software. The term freestyle machine embroidery has come to describe the process of designing art

and embellishment with a sewing machine that does not control the fabric and stitches. Computerized embroidery processes have potential as a base for freestyle embroidery, and they can be combined quite well with other fiber processes. Additionally, designs and photographs can be manipulated on a desktop computer and then translated into freestyle machine embroidery.

My process for making freestyle machine embroidery has evolved over the past twenty years. Although I know it would be interesting to experiment with the new computerized machines, I feel that I have barely touched the possibilities of what can be done with a mechanical sewing machine. My interest in the processes still feels fresh and the possibilities seem infinite.

As creative people, we often want to jump right into a process and start working with the materials. We can be so excited about the possibilities that we find it hard to slow down and learn the basics. I have designed this chapter to cover the things that I wish I had learned at the beginning, when I first started stitching seriously. If you want to learn more about setting up your studio space, or choosing a machine or accessories, turn to Your Workspace and Equipment on page 162.

Supplies

Machine sewing depends on the interaction of three components: thread, machine needle, and fabric (which dictates thread and needle type).

Fabric

The three main types of fabric are **knit**, **woven**, and **nonwoven**. Woven fabrics work much better for embroidery than do knits, which tend to stretch more. But compared to nonwoven fabrics (and films, which will be discussed later), woven fabrics can have quite a bit of stretch, or "give." Heavy fabrics can be embroidered without further support, but lightweight fabrics need to be made stiffer by the support of a backing fabric or by being stretched in an embroidery hoop.

A hoop limits the area in which you can work at any given moment and limits the area you can see. Hoops also distort the fabric and, if moved to an adjoining area of the fabric where it may cross a previously stitched area, strain or damage the stitching. However, hoops are indispensable for working with soft and flexible fabric or lightweight water-soluble films. In cases where a hoop is required, choose one with a low profile that can fit under the raised presser foot, such as a spring hoop. This type of hoop consists of a plastic outer ring and a springy metal inner ring that is tensioned in a

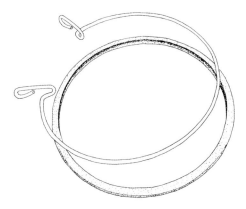

Low-profile embroidery hoop.

groove on the plastic one. To use this style of hoop, lay the plastic outer ring on a flat surface and place the fabric on top of the rim with the right side of the fabric facing up. Then squeeze the handles of the metal ring together, place it on top of the fabric, push the fabric down into the outer ring, and release the handles to secure the inner ring in the groove. The fabric will be stretched taut along the base of the hoop, where it can rest flat against the needle plate of your machine while you stitch. (A hand-embroidery hoop, by contrast, tensions the fabric across the top of the hoop.)

For most of my work, I use 10-ounce cotton-duck canvas, which is more tightly woven than plain canvas. I prefer it to denim or other heavy twill fabrics because the plain-weave structure has less stretch than a twill structure. I also prefer it to nonwoven interfacing-type fabrics, which can break down and tear or become floppy with heavy stitching. Be aware that 10-ounce canvas is not the same as "number 10" canvas. Canvas is graded either by weight per square yard or by numbers reflecting its thickness (the lower the number, the thicker or heavier it is). Ten-ounce canvas is the same canvas that beginning painters might use and is sold by the yard in art-supply stores or by mail order (see Suppliers on page 173). This type of canvas contains starch, but I do not recommend washing it out because doing so will cause the fabric to shrink and wrinkle. I prefer to paint the canvas or bond lightweight fabric to it before stitching. Alternatively, you can purchase canvas without starch or additives from Testfabrics (see Suppliers). They carry bleached army duck that seems a bit lighter weight than painters' 10-ounce canvas, and they have nice linens for embroidery, but the color is much darker than cotton canvas. Experiment to see what you like best.

I often bond lighter-weight fabrics to canvas because the smooth surface of lightweight fabric is easier to paint and draw on, photo-transfers work better on a smooth surface, or it may allow me to start a piece with a fabric collage. There are many choices for bonding agents, including fabric glue, spray adhesives, and fusible webbing. My favorite is Wonder Under, an inexpensive, fusible webbing available at most fabric stores.

Thread

Thread quality can affect the appearance of your work as well as its longevity. It can also affect your machine's performance. Threads that are fuzzy or vary in thickness can gradually push the tension disks apart and cause skipped stitches. Serger thread is notorious for causing this type of problem. Although the thread may seem economical on the purchasing end, it may necessitate getting your machine serviced more often. Also avoid threads that come on Styrofoam spools, which build up static electricity that can cause the thread to release unevenly. Note that cotton is weaker than polyester (which is why it is often spun with polyester); the strength depends on how tightly it is spun. Older cotton thread, which tends to dry out, is susceptible to frequent breaking. If you find this happening, try reviving the thread by spraying it with a little water, placing it in a plastic bag, and refrigerating it overnight.

Sewing thread comes in different weights that are designated by numbers; the finer the thread, the higher the number (but be aware that not all companies number their thread and that there can be discrepancies in the thicknesses of those that do). All weights may be used for machine embroidery, according to what you wish to achieve. For heavier-than-normal threads, you may need to use a needle with a larger eye. I like to use a fine-weight thread (50- to 60-weight) in the bobbin to reduce the amount of thread buildup on the back of the fabric. For the top thread, I generally use 40-weight, which is the size sold at most fabric stores. Thread also comes in different degrees of shine and texture.

Needles

There are many different needle types available. Knit fabrics require ballpoint needles and most woven fabrics require regular needles, or sharps. Universals are semi-ballpoint needles and are designed as "all-purpose" needles. You will have better results if you choose the needle specifically for the job. An extra-sharp point more easily penetrates heavy fabrics, such as canvas, and makes a smaller hole. Jeans/denim needles are even sharper than sharps. Because free stitching many layers of thread on heavy fabric can put a strain on the needle, a heavy needle such as a 110/18 or 100/16 may hold up better if you are new to the technique. As you gain experience, you may prefer a 90/14. Needle sizes range from 70 to 120; the finer the needle, the lower the number. Do not try to use a heavy thread in a fine needle. If the thread does not fit smoothly into the groove above the eye, skipped stitches will result.

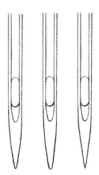

Sewing needles have different tips; shown here from left to right are standard, universal, and sharp.

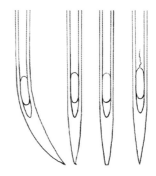

Damaged needles can cause sewing problems; shown here from left to right are a bent tip, a burr tip, a blunt tip, and a hairline crack.

Check your needle carefully. Damaged needles can harm your machine and create sewing problems. Needles with a burr or tiny hook at the tip can pluck up your fabric with each stitch, sometimes breaking or fraying the threads of the fabric. Blunt needles push down on the fabric and can even cause it to jam through the hole in your machine plate. Both can alter your sewing rhythm and cause damage to the hook of your machine. If you get a burr on the needle, you have probably hit the plate or the hook beneath the plate of your machine. Hitting the hook may also make the needle blunt, but a needle will wear down from ordinary use and become blunt even if you never hit the plate. A hairline crack above the eye of the needle is difficult to see, but it can cause your thread to catch and break. In each case, a new needle is in order.

Note: If you have sewing problems, change the needle and rethread before you blame your machine.

Sample One:
Thread-Tension Adjustment

Step 1. Cut or tear several 6–8" (15–21 cm) squares of 10-ounce canvas.

Step 2. Thread the machine with a color that contrasts with the canvas (such as black) and thread the bobbin with a color that contrasts with both the canvas and the top thread (such as red). I like to thread the bobbin with a finer-weight thread (#50) than I use in the top thread (#40). The finer-weight bobbin thread fills up the fabric less than regular-weight thread, and this allows me to stitch more thread into the piece. Some newer machines don't perform well with two different weights of thread, so experiment to see what works for yours.

Step 3. Put a darning or an embroidery foot on your machine and lower the feed dogs (the teeth under the needle plate). In normal sewing, the feed dogs move the fabric according to the stitch length or pattern chosen. However, in some older machines,

the feed dogs are stationary and a metal plate may be provided to cover the feed dogs. Some have a presser-foot regulator that can loosen the fit between the foot and the plate—refer to your machine manual to learn how to work it. If your machine has stationary feed dogs and no plate, create a temporary plate by taping a piece of an index card over the feed dogs. Poke a hole in the index card for the needle by slowly moving an unthreaded needle back and forth in the zigzag setting a few times.

Step 4. Thread the needle with the presser foot in the up position so that the thread can make full contact with the tensioning disks. Place the fabric under the foot, lower the needle, then lower the

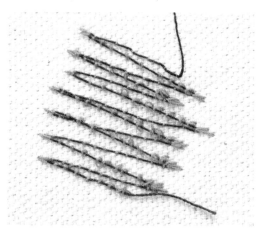

If the bobbin thread (red) shows on the surface, the tension on the top thread is tighter than the tension on the bobbin thread.

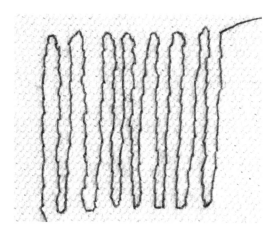

The bobbin thread will not show on the top surface of the fabric if the tension is correct.

preser foot last. It can be easy to forget to lower the foot, because it may not actually touch the fabric. If you have problems sewing, check this first—the foot needs to be lowered to engage the tension on the top thread. As you start, hold the threads at the back of the machine with your left hand to prevent them from getting tangled on the underside of the fabric. Begin sewing, gently moving the fabric backward and forward (this is generally easier than moving it from side to side) under the foot. Practice to coordinate the speed of the machine stitching with the movement of the fabric. The biggest mistake is not running the machine fast enough, which can cause you to break or damage the needle.

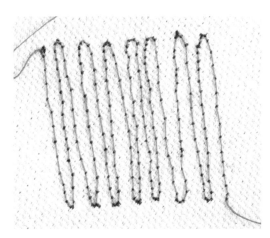

Small spots of the top thread (black) are fine on the underside of the fabric.

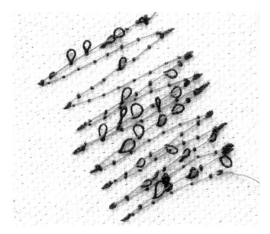

If the top thread (black) forms loops on the underside, the tension on the top thread is too loose compared to the tension on the bobbin thread.

Step 5. Examine your stitching, both on the top and on the bottom of the fabric. Are there spots or loops of the bobbin thread on the top of the fabric? If so, the tension on the top thread is tighter than the tension on the bobbin thread. The easiest way to fix this is to loosen the top tension by turning the tension dial to a lower number. Make note of the number the dial is set at before you move it so you can return to this setting for regular sewing. Ideally, the top thread and the bobbin thread should interlock within the matrix of the fabric so that the bobbin thread doesn't show on the top of the fabric and the top thread doesn't show on the bottom of the fabric. This can be difficult to achieve with embroidery, so I often accept small spots (but not loops) of the top thread on the underside. If there are loops on the underside, the tension of the top thread is looser than the tension of the bobbin thread. Correct this by turning the tension dial to a higher number.

Step 6. If the tension dial does not sufficiently fix the problem, the problem may lie in the bobbin case. Bobbin cases fit into either a vertical bobbin race (accessed through a panel in the front side of the arm of the machine) or a horizontal bobbin race (accessed under the needle plate on top of the arm). The bobbin tension is controlled by the tension spring (a metal flap that presses down on the thread as it leaves the bobbin case). The tension spring is controlled by a tiny screw. The case of a vertical bobbin race has a single screw; the case of a horizontal bobbin race has two screws, but only one controls the tension—check your manual to learn which one. Note that the tension of a horizontal-bobbin-race machine can be more finicky than a vertical-bobbin-race machine. Because of this, dealers often suggest owning two bobbin cases—one tensioned for regular sewing and the other for freestyle embroidery.

Because the screw that controls the bobbin tension can wear out more easily than the top-tension disk, always try to fix tension problems with the top tension dial first. To adjust the screw in the bobbin case, hold the case between your thumb and forefinger. Before you change the tension, make note of the position of the screwdriver groove in the screw head. Think of the groove like the hour hand of a clock face. Draw the position on a piece of masking tape that is taped to your machine for reference.

Every time you adjust the screw, hold the bobbin case in the same orientation. If the bobbin thread shows on the top of your fabric after adjusting the top tension, tighten the screw ever so slightly by turning it clockwise (to the right) the equivalent of one hour, then sew a bit to check the results. You may need to repeat this to get the result you want. If there are loops of the top thread on the bottom of your fabric, loosen the screw by turning it counterclockwise (to the left) in similar small increments. To remember which way to turn the screw, simply repeat, "righty-tighty; lefty-loosey."

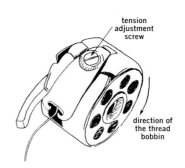

Vertical bobbin case with threaded bobbin.

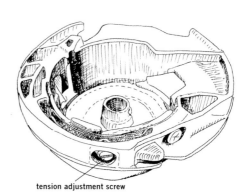

Horizontal bobbin case without threaded bobbin.

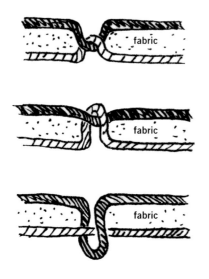

The top and bobbin threads meet in the center of the cloth when the tension is correct (top). The top tension is too tight if the bobbin thread shows on the top surface (center); the top tension is too loose if the top thread shows on the underside (bottom).

To test for normal bobbin tension, place a loaded bobbin in the case and suspend the case by holding the exiting thread by two fingers. If the bobbin case drops quickly, the tension is too loose; if the case doesn't drop at all, the tension is too tight. If the tension is correct, the bobbin case should drop in small increments with each jerk of your hand. I like the tension a little tighter so that the thread moves only a very little. Experiment to see what works best for you. Some bobbin cases include a hole in the projecting finger. Routing the bobbin thread through this hole adds tension—something that is typically done for buttonholes. I use this for most of my freestyle embroidery.

Thread tensions will need to be adjusted as you stitch because many factors affect thread tension. If you can't get your tension perfectly adjusted,

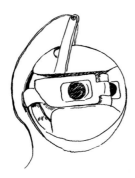

Hang the threaded bobbin from your fingers to test bobbin tension.

Route the bobbin thread through the hole in the projecting finger to increase the tension slightly.

Things That Can Affect Thread Tension

- brand of thread
- thread thickness
- thread color
- amount of thread on the spool
- type of spool
- size of spool
- age of thread
- fiber content of thread
- thickness of the fabric
- amount of paint on the fabric
- number of fabric layers to stitch through
- amount of stitching already on fabric

All of these can be corrected by a slight change in the top-tension control.

strive for small dots of the top thread showing on the underside of the fabric rather the bobbin thread showing on the top. Large loops on the underside, however, are not acceptable. If the top thread shows underneath as long dashes or loops where the stitching changes direction, try to change the direction of the fabric more gently as you sew.

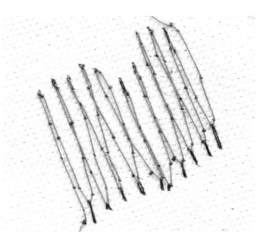

If the top thread (black) shows on the underside as dashes with each change of stitch direction, try to change the direction more gently.

Sample Two:
Understanding Stitch Direction and Fabric Distortion

Step 1. Cut or tear a piece of canvas about 7" to 8" (18 to 21 cm) wide x 9" to 10" (32 to 26 cm) long.

Step 2. Draw three rectangles on the canvas, each about 1½" (4 cm) wide x 2½" (7 cm) long.

Step 3. Stitch in the same direction as the weft of the fabric in the first rectangle, along the bias in the second rectangle, and in the same direction as the warp in the third rectangle. In each, stitch in roughly parallel strokes, stitching over and over until the rectangle is solidly stitched and the canvas is not visible through the stitches. This exercise serves two purposes: you'll learn to stitch right up to the lines you have drawn, and you'll learn the advantages and disadvantages of each stitch direction.

You'll find that your hand position is important when stitching to the edge of a shape. To give you the best control and minimize fatigue in your fingers and hands, you'll want to hold your hands in a relaxed position. Stand with your hands by your sides and notice the slight curve in your fingers when your hands are at rest. The closer you can come to replicating this curve while sewing, the more relaxed you will be and the longer you'll be able to work. If you sew with your fingers flat across the top of your work, you'll put stress on your finger joints and reduce your ability to control where each stitch is placed.

Before stitching, remove any platform, extension table, or attachment box from around the arm of your machine. Grasp your fabric gently with your right

In the top rectangle, the stitching is parallel to the weft of the canvas. The stitching caused the weft to constrict and the wrap to stretch out. In the center rectangle, the stitching is on the bias. This rectangle distorted into a parallelogram. In the bottom rectangle, the stitching is parallel to the canvas warp. In this rectangle, the warp constricted and the weft stretched out.

Fabric structure: The warp threads (vertical) are attached to the loom during the weaving process. The weft thread (horizontal) is woven into the warp and forms a selvedge edge where it changes direction (left edge). The bias (cross grain) is the diagonal line that passes across the warp and weft threads.

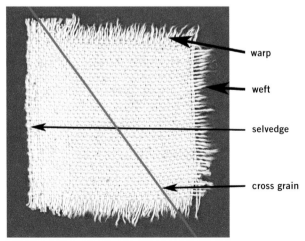

warp

weft

selvedge

cross grain

hand in front of the machine and your left hand at the back so that your left fingertips form a line under the fabric. If you touch the arm of the machine with your fingers each time you pull the fabric forward, you'll be able to produce a clean line where the stitching changes direction. Your fingers become a sort of jig or guide for controlling the stitches. If you're working with a large piece of fabric, roll it up so that you can still grasp the front and back of the stitching area for control. Sometimes I use rubber bands, office clips, or clothespins to hold a fabric roll intact while I work. You may also try turning the fabric around (so that the bottom of the image faces away from you) to stitch a particular area more easily. There are times when your left hand must hold the rolled-up fabric rather that guide the cloth at the back of the machine. In this case, brace your left fingers along the side of the free arm. There are also times when I brace my right fingers against the top or front of the free arm. Do whatever works at the moment.

Step 4. By comparing your three stitched rectangles, you will see that the one stitched on the bias has distorted differently than the two stitched along the lengthwise or crosswise grain of the fabric. You also may notice that you were able to stitch more and cover the canvas more completely in the bias-stitched rectangle. On the other hand, the rectangles stitched with the grain of the fabric have less overall distortion, but they pucker more and small bits of the canvas may have been harder to cover. Why? The bias of a fabric is the direction with the most stretch. Stitching on the bias allows the structure of the fabric to move more, causing it to distort in the process. When you stitch with the grain of the fabric, you catch the strands of the canvas over and over because the strands cannot move or stretch as easily. Instead, they may tear apart, sometimes causing bits of fiber to be pulled up to the surface. Also, when the stitch thread lies parallel to the warp or weft of the canvas, some of the stitching thread will pull down between the strands of the canvas and leave bits of the canvas exposed. When you stitch on the bias, however, the thread always travels over the top of the fabric warp and weft, remaining above the surface of the canvas and covering it more readily. Even if the needle enters on top of a warp or weft strand, it is less likely to compromise the fabric's strength because the thread is not pulled down into the matrix of the weave.

If you sew with your fingers flat across the top of your work, you'll stress your joints and have less control of the stitches.

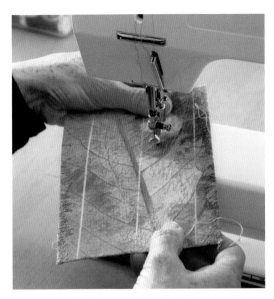

For best results, stitch with your right hand in front and your left hand in back.

Line up the fingers of your left hand and use them as a guide against the back of the arm.

If your fabric is large, roll it up so that you can still grasp it in the front and back.

At times, your left fingers may need to act as a brace along the side of the arm.

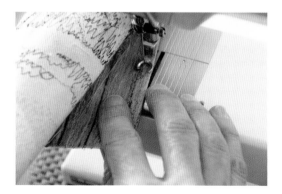

When needed, brace your right fingers against the top or front of the arm.

I have discovered that when stitching with the grain of the fabric, I have difficulty in covering the edges that run parallel to the stitches. Stitching on the bias makes this easier and means that all of the edges are covered with stitches that run at a similar angle.

Regardless of the direction you stitch, your stitching adds more fiber (thread) to the structure of the fabric, causing it to expand in the direction opposite to the direction of the stitches. Additionally, each stitch pulls the fabric fibers a little closer together. For more on fabric distortion, see page 170.

Each stitch direction has its advantages and disadvantages. If you have covered your ground canvas with a beautiful fabric or have interesting visual information that you do not want to distort or cover, you may prefer to stitch less heavily so that the fabric shows more (see page 24). In this case, it may make more sense to stitch with the grain of the fabric. If, on the other hand, you want the stitched surface to be all that is visible, stitch on the bias.

I stitch most of my work on the bias (though not necessarily at a true 45-degree angle—more on that later) because I put a lot of thread in my pieces. In the past, I allowed the pieces to distort from rectangles to extreme parallelograms. Because the shape changes spoke of my embroidery process, I did not trim the finished pieces into rectangles. Instead, I would paint the canvas so that the images were elongated in the direction that I planned to stitch, knowing that the shapes would be corrected by distortion as I stitched.

I now cut the canvas for my pieces on the bias. If I stitch in a direction parallel to or at a very slight angle to the sides of the fabric, the stitching ends up on the bias to the fabric. Even with this approach, some horizontal distortion occurs, which must be considered before the stitching begins. When stitching parallel to the edges, it can be difficult to completely cover the edges with stitches. To obscure the problem, I work stitches at an angle to the edges first, then cover these with stitches that are parallel to the edges.

An important property of line as a design element in artwork is direction. This includes shapes that appear as lines as well as lines made by mark making (in this case, lines of stitches). A horizontal line imparts feelings of rest and calm. A vertical line implies power, strength, and stability. A diagonal line is associated with movement and action. For this reason, different styles are created by different stitching directions. Stitching diagonally on the picture plane creates a more dynamic system of mark making and can add visual interest. Stitches made either vertically or horizontally on the picture plane may appear less active, but they can be excellent for creating atmosphere and mood, as in Anne Eckley's piece *Where the Townhouses Were* (see page 28). But be aware that if you stitch heavily in more than one direction, a piece can buckle or distort into an odd shape. *Identifying the Species Veloxvermis refesceus (Red Speedworms)* is such a case (see page 29). Light stitching may prevent a piece from buckling as much, particularly if the piece is small. Light stitching also will emphasis the stitches as marks because each line of stitches is more distinct.

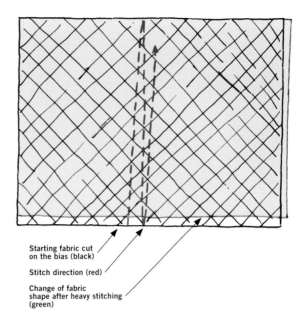

Starting fabric cut on the bias (black)

Stitch direction (red)

Change of fabric shape after heavy stitching (green)

Bias-cut fabric with vertical stitching. The black outline shows the shape and grain of the fabric cut on the bias. After stitching heavily parallel to the sides of the fabric (shown in red), the fabric becomes a bit shorter and a bit wider (shown in green).

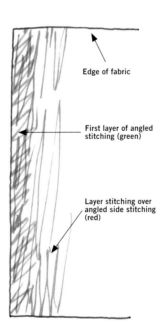

Edge of fabric

First layer of angled stitching (green)

Layer stitching over angled side stitching (red)

To completely cover the edges, angle the first layer of stitches along the side edges of a piece (shown in green).

River Stones, Robert Stefl and Carol Shinn 1995.
In 1995, I collaborated on several pieces with photographer Robert Stefl. Robert printed his black-and-white photos onto heavy cotton twill, using a liquid emulsion in the darkroom. Because the photograph was so beautiful on the fabric, I chose to leave much of the fabric visible. I wanted there to be contrast between the embroidery and the photograph, but I also wanted the embroidery to be integrated into the image. I chose to think of the embroidery as hand coloring the black-and-white image, but I stitched only part of each piece with color. This posed difficulties with stitched areas that were prone to distortion, especially on the twill fabric. I knew that I could not block and steam the piece after stitching without causing the photograph to crack and chip. But by reinforcing the back of the piece with canvas and not stitching as heavily as usual, I was able to minimize the distortion. Stitching less heavily also helped integrate the two mediums.

Detail of *River Stones*.

Left: I began *Exit 242* with a photo collage. Behind the collage is the photocopy I made of the collage, marked with an angled grid. When I hand copied the image onto canvas marked with a perpendicular grid, I intentionally distorted the image by copying the shapes in relation to the grid.

Below: Here the piece has been painted and covered with an initial layer of stitches. The piece is just beginning to distort from stitching, but the angled image is not yet corrected by stitching. Note that the angle of things in the painted image is in the same direction as the stitching. The change of the angle is most evident in the exit sign. Notice also how I have added definition to the mirror that was missing in the photo.

Exit 242, Carol Shinn 1994, 25" x 34" (64 x 87 cm). Machine stitching on fabric. Photographer: Kelley Kirkpatrick. Gregg Museum of Art & Design, North Carolina State University, gift of the 1993–1994 Friends of the Gallery. Given in memory of Shelby Parker.

By the time the piece was completed, definition also was added to the background hillside and to the highway. In the completed piece, the angles have shifted and the fabric has become a parallelogram.

Where the Townhouses Were, Anne Eckley 2004, 8" x 10"
(21 x 26 cm). Machine stitching on fabric. Photographer:
Rick Wells. Collection of Mr. and Mrs. Jim Boyd.
Vertical stitches can create atmosphere and mood.

Identifying the Species Veloxvermis refesceus (Red Speed-worms), Carol Shinn 1988, 10½" x 16¼" (27 x 42 cm).
Photographer: Carol Shinn. Private collection.

Stitching heavily in more than one direction can cause
severe distortion.

Large stitches create more energy.

Small stitches offer more control but less energy.

Consider the size of your stitches. The larger they are, the more they will show up as distinct marks. Stitch size has nothing to do with the stitch length on your machine (you disabled the feed dogs when they were lowered). In freestyle embroidery, stitch length is controlled by how fast you move the fabric in relation to how fast you run the machine. The faster you move the fabric, the larger the stitch length. If you run the machine too slowly, you will hit the plate with your needle and either break or blunt it. Although you may have less accuracy in your work, a larger and more impulsive stitch can be exciting as part of a style, as long as you use the same kind of stitch throughout a piece. Compare the energy of the large loose stitches of the cloud on page 30 to the smaller and more controlled stitches in the cloud above.

Larger stitches tend to draw in the fabric more than small stitches do. I often end up with some areas having bigger stitches than other areas. This can be a problem with some areas contracting more than others. I can usually iron this out with effort; it all becomes part of the give and take of the process. If the problem remains, I will cut darts and resew an area that has bubbled (see Troubleshooting on page 69).

Caring for Your Machine

Proper care of your machine, including oiling, cleaning, and annual checkups can ensure smooth sewing and prevent breakdowns.

Oil

If your machine is noisier than usual, it probably needs oil, but try not to wait that long. Oil it on a regular basis. (Some new machines are made with nylon and other high-tech materials and do not use oil.) Use high-quality oil designed for sewing machines, not generic oil such as WD30 or 10W40. Caustic elements in these oils can damage your machine. When oiling, gently rock the hand wheel and put a small drop of oil anywhere that metal rubs against metal. Refer to your machine manual for oiling locations. Use a little, not a lot.

The most important place to oil is around the bobbin hook. To begin, remove the bobbin and bobbin case and brush out all the collected lint and thread fragments. Then take out your hook (the part that wraps around the bobbin case), if it comes out, and run a little oil along the outside curved edge. Not all hooks are removable; refer to your manual if you're in doubt. After oiling, sew on a scrap of fabric for a minute to remove any extra oil. If you sew a lot, it is good to oil the machine every day or after every fourth bobbin of thread.

The Hook

The hook fits around the bobbin case and helps make each stitch. In most machines these are removable, but not in all. Sometimes a break in sewing rhythm can cause the needle to come down at the wrong time and hit the hook. This not only creates a burr or blunts the needle, but it can also create a burr on the hook. Periodically take the hook out, if you can. If you can feel a burr on the hook, have it filed professionally. Don't try to do this yourself—the hook is easily damaged and expensive to replace. If the hook can't be removed, have it examined as part of a routine checkup.

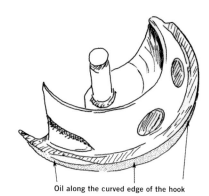

Oil along the curved edge of the hook

Curved edge of the hook in a removable vertical bobbin race.

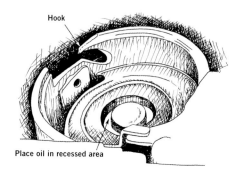

Hook

Place oil in recessed area

Oil the recessed area of a horizontal or drop-in bobbin race.

Motor Brushes

Motor brushes are actually not brushes, but small cylinders of carbon set on springs. These cylinders wear down as the machine is run—the more you sew, the faster they wear away. It is important to replace them before they wear down to the spring. If the springs start to rub, the motor will be damaged and need replacing. (Some cannot be replaced; those that can will cost you a bundle.) It's a good idea to have these checked annually. If your machine stops dead, don't fiddle with motor brushes yourself—you may ruin the motor.

Troubleshooting

- If your thread wads up in a tangle every time you start, make sure you have threaded the machine with the presser foot up. Then put the presser foot down. Start the machine with the needle down in the fabric. Also, hold both your top and your bottom thread at the back of the machine as you start to stitch. Make sure you have lowered the foot (even though the foot may not actually touch the fabric) to engage the top-thread tension. Check to see that you have positioned the bobbin correctly. The bobbin case should turn clockwise when you pull on the thread.

- If you are getting lots of bent or broken needles, it may mean you're moving the fabric too fast for the speed at which you're running the machine. Try running the machine a little faster.

- If the thread keeps breaking, try another thread; you may be using old thread or thread that has been spun unevenly. Check to see whether the thread has come off the spool and has gotten wound around the thread holder. Check to see that the thread is running freely through the eye of the needle. Replace your needle; it may have a hairline crack that is catching the thread, or it may have gotten gummed up. Check to see that you put the bobbin in the bobbin case in the right direction. Lastly, check to see whether your top tension is too tight.

- If the fabric keeps getting pushed down into the machine, the needle is probably blunt; try replacing it. This can also happen if you have overstitched a small area and have not stitched much around it.

- If the bobbin thread shows on the top of your piece, you may need to loosen the top-tension disk (adjust to a lower number) or tighten the bobbin tension (turn the screw on the bobbin case slightly to the right). If the bobbin thread only shows when you change the direction of your stitches, try changing direction more gently or more slowly.

- If the top thread makes loops on the back of your piece, you may need to tighten the top-tension disks (adjust to a higher number) or loosen the bobbin tension (turn the screw to the left). Remember, "righty-tighty, lefty-loosey." If you see loops only where you have changed stitch direction, try using a less jerky motion when you change stitch direction.

- If the stitched surface has areas that look like a washboarded dirt road, the fabric beneath has pulled up in ridges. You can disguise the problem by carefully directing the needle into the tops of the ridges and across the valleys.

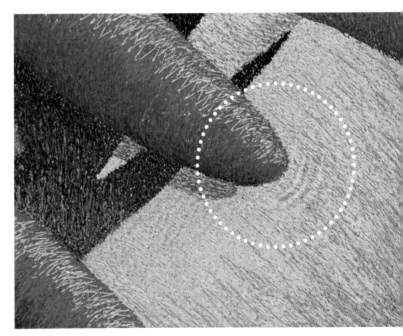

Fabric that has been pulled up in ridges will cause partial rings of color change, as near the tip of the speedworm in this detail of *Identifying the Species Veloxvermis refesceus (Red Speedworms)*.

Chapter Two:
Color Mixing

"You learn how to make your work by *making your work*."
–David Bayles and Ted Orland, from *Art and Fear: Observations on the Perils (and Rewards) of Artmaking*

In this chapter, I offer exercises to help you enrich your work with layers of thread in multiple colors. For these exercises, you'll need cotton canvas (preferably 10-ounce duck), thread in a variety of colors, acrylic paint, a small brush that is stiff and flat, and colored pencils.

Exercise One:
Layering Thread Colors

I encourage you to mix colors by layering the thread, not by using solid blocks of single colors. Single colors are bold, but they are visually understood so quickly that the piece may soon lose interest, both for you and for viewers of your work. Think of billboards: by necessity they are understood quickly. But wouldn't you like to have people look at your work a little longer? This exercise involves the standard terms used in basic color theory—see page 165 for explanations.

A practical reason for mixing colors is that you may not have the exact color of thread that you need. Because there are gaps in the value and hue spectrums of commercially available thread, the exact color may not even exist. I have become particularly

aware of the gaps when I try to organize threads to depict shaded skies that change from darker to lighter blues. A mix of colors can visually disguise these gaps and create the overall color you're after.

Thread colors also change with fashion. When I first learned that manufacturers change and discontinue thread colors, I panicked. "What will I do without this specific color? How can it be gone forever!" I must constantly compensate for color discontinuations and so must you; your work will be richer for it.

Paint a square in a medium-value color, then draw lines to create four equal quarters that will be stitched with different colors of thread.

I created this color gradation by changing the thread thirty times. If you look closely, you will see tiny bits of rose, green, and other colors mixed in with the more expected colors.

a) Stitch the entire square with a color that matches the paint.

b) Stitch a second layer in each quadrant, using a lighter value in the first; a complement in the second; a grayed, duller color in the third; and an analogous color in the fourth.

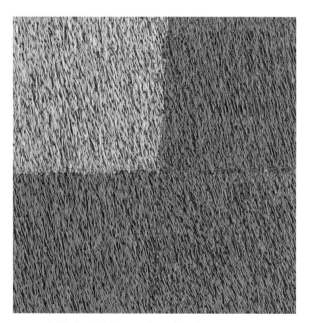

c) Stitch a third layer using colors that appear to be a mix of the original and the second layer colors.

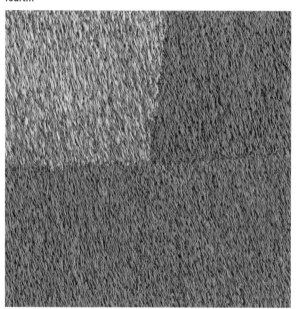

d) Stitch a final layer of the basic color across the entire initial square so that only bits of the other colors pop through the thread matrix.

Step 1. Cut or tear an 8" (21 cm) square of canvas.

Step 2. Draw a large square in the center of the canvas and paint it a medium-value color (value refers to the lightness and darkness of a color) using acrylic paint that is mixed with water to the consistency of thick cream. When the paint is dry, draw two dark lines over it to divide the initial square into equal quarters.

Step 3. Using a top thread color that matches the paint and a bobbin thread that is medium-value gray or similar to your paint color, lightly stitch the large initial square all over along the bias. (I use 50-weight thread in the bobbin.)

Step 4. Lightly layer the other colors in the quadrants so that the threads build up gradually. Stitch lighter values of the basic color in one quadrant. In the second quadrant, stitch a complementary color (a hue directly across the color wheel) of a similar value as the basic color. In the third quadrant, stitch gray or a duller version of the basic color. In the last square, stitch an analogous color (a color that is a neighbor on the color wheel) of the same value as your original color. Stitch a third layer in each quadrant with colors that appear to be a mix of the original color and the second layer color in each quadrant. With each layer, aim for an even pattern of stitches across the surface of the fabric.

Step 5. When each painted square is nearly covered, stitch a final layer in the basic color so that only bits of the other colors pop through the thread matrix. Take a minute to note which color combination appears the smoothest or most evenly colored. Which appears the most textured? This exercise illustrates how the eye sees value contrasts first, then hues.

Step 6. Look closely at the density of the stitches at the edges of each quadrant. Whenever you change direction of the stitching, a point is formed. The areas around the points may appear less densely stitched than the center of the shape. You can fill in the gaps between the points by adding more stitches along the edges.

To finish your sample, heavily steam-press it from the back, pulling the piece flat as you do so. Never iron the front of your work.

Stitching up to the edge of a shape or to the edge of a piece creates pointed lines. The red lines represent the first layer of stitches. To fill in around the points and make the stitching appear more even, more stitches may be needed along the edges, as shown in purple.

Exercise Two:
Understanding Gradation

Shading, or creating a gradation, is achieved when one color gradually shifts to another. A painter might accomplish this by gradually mixing one paint color into the other. Shading also can be done with stitching, though the transition area—with the two colors blended or hatched into each other—can look more textured than the solid-color areas. This texture can add interest because the stitches are more visible. Sometimes, however, a smoother gradation will look richer and will look more convincing in realistic work. In the examples on page 38, you can see how the addition of just one more color can smooth a color gradation.

The following exercise will give you experience in gradations made in different stitch directions as well as mixing thread colors between complementary colors. For more on color complements, see page 165.

Step 1. Cut or tear two 8" (21 cm) squares of canvas.

Step 2. On each piece of fabric, draw a rectangle about 5" x 2" (13 x 5 cm), aligning the rectangle with the grain of the fabric on one and aligning the rectangle along the bias of the fabric on the other. You will stitch each sample along the bias of the fabric, but because the rectangles are drawn differently, your stitches will mix differently. On the rectangle drawn with the grain of the fabric, you will stitch diagonal to the rectangle. On the rectangle drawn on the bias of the fabric, you will stitch parallel to the short edge of the rectangle.

Step 3. Divide each rectangle widthwise into five equal sections.

Step 4. Choose a basic color (hue) and its complement—such as blue and orange. Mix a batch of acrylic paint for these two colors, aiming for the consistency of thick cream. Mix enough of each color so that you can paint six small rectangles and have a little left over. On each piece of canvas, paint the first section of the rectangle with one color (blue) and paint the last section with the other color (orange).

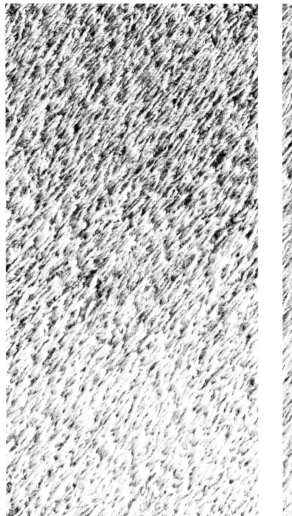

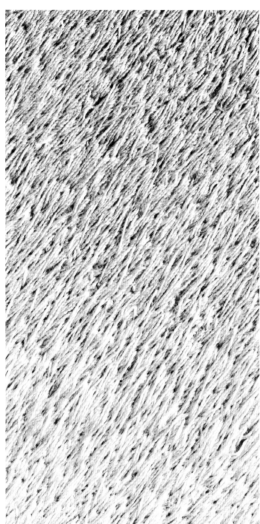

This gradation from light to dark is made with just two values of blue.

This gradation, made with three values of blue, has a smoother look.

Choose thread colors that match the painted rectangles.

Step 5. Using half of each remaining batch of paint, mix a color that appears halfway between the base hue and its complement. This will be a medium-value grayish color. Paint the center section on each piece of fabric with this color.

Step 6. Finally, mix each basic hue and each complement with the grayish color to create interme-diate colors (teal and brown) and paint the remaining sections with these colors. Each piece of fabric will have a row of painted colors with a complement color at each end and three steps of color in between.

Step 7. Choose five colors of thread that match the painted rectangles as closely as possible, paying attention to value as well as hue.

First layer of stitches on the rectangle drawn with the grain of the fabric.

First layer of stitches on the rectangle drawn on the bias of the fabric.

Step 8. Using the thread that matches each complementary color (blue and orange) stitch lightly across half of the rectangle, stitching more heavily at the end painted with that color and thinning it out to less thread near the center, crossing into the middle sections so that the two colors just touch at the center.

Gray is added to the center of the rectangle drawn with the grain of the fabric.

Gray is added to the center of the rectangle drawn on the bias of the fabric.

Step 9. Stitch the middle grayish color in the center three sections, stitching more heavily in the center section and more lightly in each adjacent section. Allow very sparse stitching to touch the inner edge of the outermost (blue and orange) sections.

Finished rectangle drawn with the grain of the fabric.

A bit of rust smoothes the transition between the orange and brown.

Finished rectangle drawn on the bias of the fabric.

Step 10. Stitch the remaining two colors (teal and brown), starting in the correspondingly colored sections and gradually moving into the center section, sparsely overlapping the two colors in the very center and stitching sparsely halfway into the end sections.

Step 11. Take a minute to evaluate your work. Make sure that there is the same amount of thread across the entire fabric surface and that the edges look as heavily stitched as the center. Also check that the color gradation is becoming smooth. If you see a sharp jump between two of the colors, you may need to add

another hue to smooth out the transition. In making these samples, I added a light rust thread to make a better transition between the orange and brown.

Step 12. Using these five colors, stitch layer upon layer. Feel free to add other colors that fit into the gradation. You also may want to stitch bits of other colors of the same value to add visual interest. When the painted fabric is nearly covered, look carefully to assess the evenness of shading, and finish with the end colors or any of the five that will finalize your smooth shading.

Yellow Room, Carol Shinn 2005, 22¼" x 13½" (57 x 35 cm). Machine stitching on fabric. Photographer: Carol Shinn. Private collection.

This piece started with a photo of a cluttered café house in Phoenix. I used Photoshop to clean up the clutter in the photo so that I could elaborate on the color gradations to make each wall and doorway more intriguing. Gradations are among the best tools for adding color interest to artwork. Gradations, which can be between any two or more colors, encourage the eye to travel around the piece.

Veloxvermis sulphurostris (Sulphur-nosed Speedworms),
Carol Shinn 1988, 9¾" x 15½" (25 x 40 cm). Machine
stitching on fabric. Photographer: Carol Shinn.
Private collection.

Exercise Three:
Planning and Stitching a Complete Design

When making samples, I often think up a design
problem to help expand my abilities. Technique is
only one skill in making successful art. Design and
color skills need to be practiced as much as technique.
In this exercise, we'll study the illusion of transparency within the confines of a simplified design.

I first tried to convey transparency with thread by
using contrasting thin layers of stitches to represent
steamy vapors in a piece titled *Veloxvermis sulphurostris (Sulphur-nosed Speedworms)*. (The piece

describes an imaginary life form called speedworms.
I saw speedworms as a genus with many species,
each living in a unique environment.) This sketchy
quality was fine for the spontaneous depiction of an
on-the-spot recording of the species, but smoother
transitional colors would have looked more realistic.

In the following exercise, we will stitch the entire
surface of the canvas and treat the layered shapes like
pieces of glass. To practice even shading, we will aim
for shapes with smooth, consistent stitch textures.

Step 1. To make a shape appear transparent, it must partially overlap another shape. It is important that the top shape (Shape A) not be completely surrounded by the back shape (Shape B); extend Shape A past the edge of Shape B. The color of Shape A is affected by the color of Shape B behind it. For example, if Shape A is yellow and Shape B is blue, the area where they overlap will appear green (a mix of yellow and blue). I like to think of the front and back shapes (yellow and blue) as parents and the color created where they overlap (green) as the child that holds qualities from both parents.

If the mixed (child) color appears to have more of one of the two original (parent) colors, that color will appear to be in front or on top of the other. In the example below, a golden-yellow bar crosses three rusty-red bars. The intersection of the two colors on the left contains more of the rusty-red, which causes the red bar to appear as though it were on top of the yellow bar. The opposite occurs on the right, where the intersecting color has more yellow in it, causing the yellow bar to appear on top. The intersection in the center has equal amounts of yellow and rusty red and neither appears to be on top.

On paper, draw some simple sketches of transparent overlapping shapes. Plan a composition that measures about 6" x 8" (15 x 21 cm). Plan at least one transparent overlapping shape in your design as well as gradations and other types of color mixing. Plan to stitch the entire surface of the cloth—you'll need to

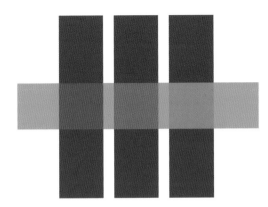

The color of the overlapping shapes will determine whether the shape appears to be on the top or bottom. By carefully choosing opaque colors, I have made the yellow horizontal bar appear transparent to different degrees as it crosses the red bars.

consider what fills the background behind the shapes. To begin, keep the composition simple. To create an interesting composition, ask yourself the following start-up questions:

- How do the shapes and spaces relate to each other? Are the shapes sparsely or densely positioned? Are they positioned in an ordered or a random pattern? Do the shapes take up more or less of the composition than the surrounding area?
- Would it be more interesting if one or more of the shapes ran off the edge?
- Are there too many different kinds of shapes in the design? Would similar shapes help unify the design?
- Are the shapes too much the same? Would it help to vary their sizes? Would it help to further change or vary their colors?
- Are the contours of the spaces between the shapes interesting? Think of yourself as an ant walking between your shapes. Would your journey be interesting?

Decide whether you'll want to stitch vertically or horizontally to the image or along the bias (see Exercise 2). Remember that a rectangular piece will distort into a parallelogram with bias stitching. If you wish, cut your square or rectangle on the bias and plan to stitch vertically or horizontally to the image. Keep in mind that a bias-cut edge may fray and ruffle. You can reduce this by backing the fabric with Wonder Under and a lightweight nonwoven interfacing. For a more in-depth explanation of distortion and stitch direction, see page 170.

Step 2. Tear or cut a piece of canvas to match the size of your drawing, then sketch the composition in pencil on the canvas. Mix acrylic paints (to the consistency of thick cream) for each color in the composition. If you want to use the color of the canvas in your composition, mix some paint that color, too. Paint the fabric with an even layer of paint so that when the paint dries, the entire surface of the fabric will be equally stiff.

Step 3. Decide which direction you'll stitch—vertically, horizontally, diagonally to the left, or diagonally to the right (keep in mind that you'll be able to stitch more densely if you stitch along the bias). Using a

Design and paint the entire surface of the canvas with acrylic paint.

A bias-cut sample that has begun to be stitched vertically.

Partially completed piece with green, violet, and light blue added for complexity.

colored pencil, draw a series of faint parallel lines about 1" to 2" (2.5 to 5 cm) apart across the canvas in the direction you plan to stitch. Use these lines to guide your first layer of stitches and help you maintain a consistent angle. Erase the lines as much as possible after the first layer of stitches so that the pencil coloring won't bleed or travel up through the thread (see page 61).

For this exercise, you will stitch in the same direction throughout the piece. That's because a piece will buckle and be difficult to iron flat if you stitch in different directions. Some artists use this buckling to their advantage, but if you want to experiment with undulating effects, do so with another prepared canvas.

It may be difficult to hold the canvas as you stitch next to the edge or into a corner. One of my students devised a perfect solution for this problem: stitch one line to the corner, then pull the piece out from the machine and clip the threads, leaving 6" (15 cm) tails (shown in the photo at center left). Hold onto these tails to help stabilize the fabric when you stitch near the corner.

Step 4. Consider additional thread colors to give more life to the composition. I added green at the top of the blue area that graded to violet at the bottom. I also added light blue along the edge of the cream-colored shape. Keep each layer thin and build up layer by layer, elaborating as you see fit. You want to have the option of adding colors until you are close to finishing the stitching. Remember to stitch up to the edges of each shape, adding extra stitches if necessary. You can also rip out the thread in some areas to remove shapes or colors that aren't working. It's also possible to repaint an area, as long as the paint is well thinned and the painted area is stitched.

When you're finished stitching, clip the top threads. Turn the piece over and give the bottom threads a gentle tug to pull the ends of the top threads to the underside, then clip the bottom threads. Don't worry if a thread pops out on the front. Any extra loose ends can be clipped again just before a piece is framed. The only exception is when a loose end might ruin the effect of an exacting detail. In that

Completed sample.

case, I begin and end the stitching of an area by stitching in place (not moving the fabric) for a few stitches to lock the threads before I clip them.

Step 5. Lastly, steam-press the back of the piece, pulling the fabric in the direction in which it is naturally stretching. This will help it lie flatter. Never iron the front of the piece—doing so will cause the threads to flatten and mash together.

This collage is made from three photographs. The photo of the clouds was copied onto a transparency and placed over the other two. Interestingly, the clouds appear to be behind the other photographs even though they are the top layer.

Agave, Carol Shinn 1998, 7½" x 11" (19 x 28 cm).
Machine stitching on fabric. Photographer: Carol Shinn.
Private collection.

This piece was stitched using the collage at left to exploit
the effect of transparency. I exaggerated the colors of the
layers to help distinguish them from each other.

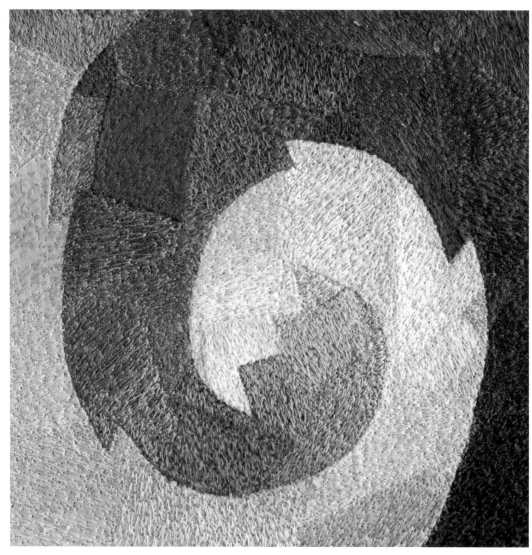

Sample using a figure/ground reversal.

More Samples

You will gain more experience if you try to stretch your abilities with each sample or piece you create. Explore various design problems. The example shown above started as a collage of fabrics forming a **figure/ground reversal**. This term is used to describe designs in which it's impossible to tell which shape represents the background and which represents the front form. The classic example of this problem is the image of two faces in profile with the space between them forming a vase. In my composition, I arranged the fabric scraps to shift in value from light at the center to dark at the edges, working with fabrics of different colors but roughly matched in value along the gradation. Stitching helped even out the values, while increasing the variety and intensity of the colors. This is a good exercise for training your eye to see the nuances of thread colors and their relative values.

Look through a general design book such as *Design Basics* (see Recommended Books on page 172) to get ideas for other samples. For example, make a study of colored and textured paper scraps from magazines. The magazine-scrap collage at right formed the foundation for the stitched sample below, which is a study of **lost and found contours**. This term describes edges and shapes that blend or partially disappear into adjoining areas because they share a similar color or value. In my stitched version, I altered the colors to enhance contrast in some areas and to decrease contrast in others.

Above: This collage was made with parts of images collected from magazines. It was designed to explore lost and found contours.

Below: Stitched sample based on the collage above.

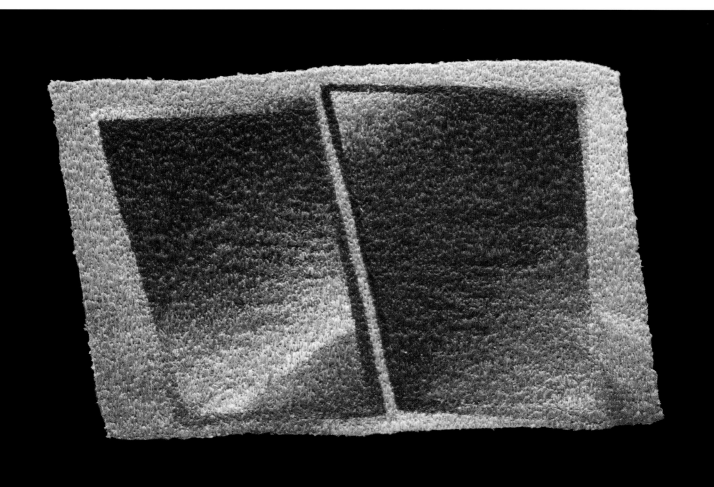

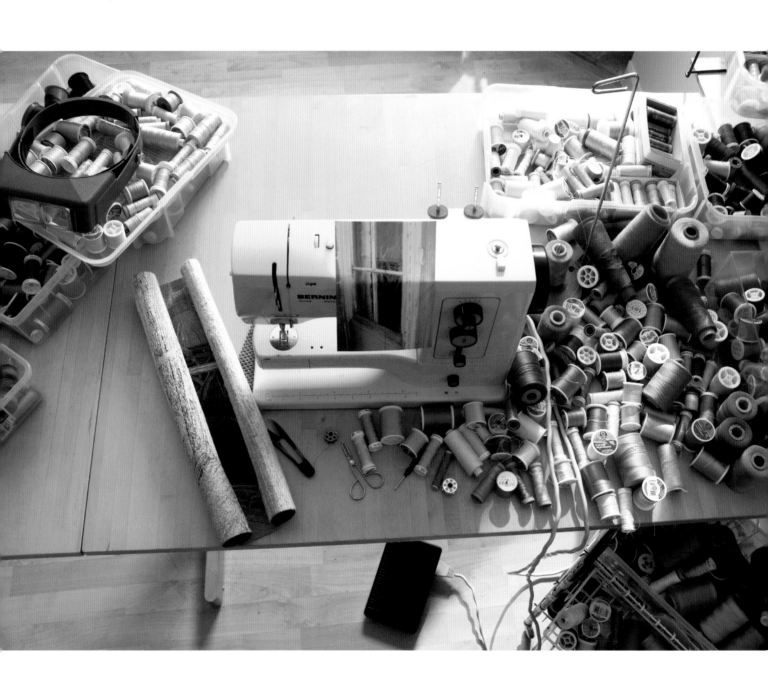

Chapter Three:
My Process for Making an Embroidery

"Art is the only way to run away without leaving home."
—Twila Tharp, contemporary dancer and choreographer

A large portion of the information that we experience each day is visual. Although we have always been visual animals, we now are bombarded with images from books, magazines, television, computers, billboards, store windows, catalogs, and more. We become jaded. In our day-to-day lives we treat our visual world like background static, and it becomes more difficult to find things that capture and keep our attention. How can we as artists hope to hold the attention of an audience? Art is communication; it is important to consider what we want to say and how we can convey it in a way that won't be dismissed. That is the challenge.

Choosing a Subject and Designing a Piece

How does an artist come up with ideas, especially new ones? An artist can't afford to sit around and wait for inspiration to strike. Very rarely do ideas just "pop" into the artist's mind—instead, they develop during the process of working. The process begins with clarifying the limitations of the specific artwork about to be made, including the limitations of the chosen materials and the maker's skill. Part of the impetus for making things comes from the desire to expand these limits and that can only happen through the process of working. Not everything you make will be extraordinary, but every piece *will* increase your knowledge for future work.

Most pieces begin with a period of brainstorming about new challenges. This is the time to ask yourself what ideas you want to convey. Are the subject matter and the message the same, or do you want to use the subject to convey an additional message? Do you want to try new materials or techniques? Are there different ways to lay out the design? Can you use your personal viewpoint to make the piece more interesting?

To find your personal viewpoint, identify the things that are most important in your work. Ask yourself what you like or don't like in other artists' works.

When working, I always tape a small photo of the image I am stitching to my machine. This allows me to quickly take in the whole image and helps me think about the original colors of the photograph as well as think about color changes.

Your own viewpoint is extremely important, but your work will be stronger if you also consider what a viewer will be able to understand. Are you speaking in code or a common language? Will you use cultural references and symbols?

Try understatement. Suggestion and nuance may be more interesting than the most literal presentation. The viewer can always imagine the more dramatic and the more intense. But if the artwork depicts the pinnacle, the most dramatic coloring, or the most intense moment, nothing is left for the viewer to imagine. On the other hand, exaggeration may seem fresher and may focus the viewer's attention. Think about how your work could be both understated and exaggerated. As artists, our role is to open the imagination of those around us; in the effort to communicate, we open and expand our own imaginations.

For quite some time, my point of view has focused on the surfaces, colors, and light qualities of places and objects that are significant to me. I concentrate not only on tactile surfaces but also on the moods

The photograph of summer clouds that I used.

The photograph of a chair that I chose for *End of the Season*.

End of the Season, Carol Shinn 2004, 18½" x 15¼" (47 x 39 cm). Machine stitching on fabric. Photographer: Carol Shinn. Collection of Tom and Jeanann Fausser.

evoked by these things and places. I control and isolate information about a subject by depicting it from a particular vantage point and by manipulating color and light.

For example, I'll review my thought process in creating *End of the Season* (see page 55). In 2004, I began a series of embroideries featuring chairs. I wanted each to suggest a story. I took fourteen photographs of an interesting chair with wooden slats to compare the mood caught by different angles and distances. I initially chose one that emphasized the weathered wood, which inspired me to create a feeling of time past, but then I realized it didn't say enough. The photo, shot from above with the chair's back turned, felt more like it had moved away from the "present" and also emphasized the rhythmic pattern of the cast shadow. Crowding the chair into the top of the picture plane put it into a more dynamic location and gave me space to develop a more dramatic staging. I decided what had "passed" was the summer season, when people play or relax in the sand. To add to the feeling of summer and passing time, I chose to add the image of a typical summer cloud from my photo file. I chose to use it as a transparency to suggest that both the chair and the cloud were passing memories.

The rest of this chapter follows my process for making an embroidery. Like *End of the Season*, *Window with Aloe* (which is part of a series on windows and doors; see page 67) focuses on the transitory nature of life. Instead of using transparency to evoke the passing of time as I did in *End of the Season*, I contrasted a brightly colored living plant with the weathered exterior of a building. The composition of leaves actively pointing in many directions against the mostly vertical, quieter lines of the wood adds to the contrast.

Ink-Jet Heat Transfer of Photographic Images

There are a number of ways to transfer photographic images onto fabric, but many have become obsolete since the advent of heat-transfer paper and ink-jet printers. Currently, a popular way to print an image onto fabric is to saturate the fabric with Bubble Jet Set (available from craft and quilting shops), iron the treated fabric onto freezer paper, cut the fabric to fit your ink-jet printer bed, and print. This method is easy and allows the fabric to retain its flexibility, but the size of the print is limited by the size of your printer. The colors end up less vibrant and less defined than in the initial photograph, which can make it more difficult to discern the edges of the shapes as you stitch.

I prefer the crisp and vibrant images I can get from heat-transfer paper (available from office-supply stores and Dharma Trading Company; see Suppliers on page 173). This product also allows me to piece together larger images, and the transfer adds more body to the fabric. Dharma's product is easy to use, inexpensive, and has given me consistent, good results.

Step 1. Create a design using any technique—photography, drawing, painting, collage, etc.—and scan it into your computer. I use Adobe Photoshop to make alterations and to resize my photographs. In addition to enlarging my images, I typically make them a little taller in relation to their width to compensate for the distortion that will result from stitching. I also lighten the image and increase the contrast so that it will be easier to see the details when I begin to stitch. If you want the final image to have the same left-right orientation as the original, you will need to reverse the image in your computer (in Photoshop, go to Image/Rotate Canvas/Flip Canvas Horizontal). Most printers are capable of the same reversal function, which may be called "mirror image."

The paper can be purchased in 8½" x 11" (22 x 28 cm) or 11" x 17" (28 x 43 cm) sizes. If your image is larger than your printer can handle, divide it into smaller sections. Most of my designs fit on two sheets of 11" x 17" (28 x 43 cm) paper or four sheets of 8½" x 11" (22 x 28 cm) paper. I crop the image two or four times, depending on the size of my paper, capturing a different section of the image for each printing and allowing at least ¼" (6 mm) overlap on each part.

Step 2. Trim the border from each printed sheet of heat-transfer paper, then piece them together. Use small bits of masking tape (which is better able to withstand the heat of an iron than clear plastic tape) to hold the backs of the pieces together.

Step 3. Measure a piece of white or very light-colored cotton-polyester broadcloth to fit your image, allowing about ½" (1 cm) extra around all sides. (You'll need opaque transfer paper if you want to print on a dark fabric.) Cut the fabric along the grain. Next, cut a piece of Wonder Under just slightly smaller than the broadcloth, then measure and cut a piece of canvas slightly smaller than the image. I cut the canvas roughly on the bias (the angle does not have to be exactly 45 degrees to the grain).

I have found that a heat-transfer image ironed onto a smooth lightweight fabric such as broadcloth is sharper than if ironed directly onto canvas. Broadcloth isn't stiff enough to work on without an embroidery hoop, so to get the smoothness of the lightweight fabric and the stiffness of the canvas, I bond them together with Wonder Under (available at most fabric stores).

Step 4. Place the broadcloth on an ironing surface. Rather than using a typical ironing board that has foam padding, which can cause the image to shift during the ironing process, use a sturdy table or other hard, flat surface. I wrap a folded bed sheet around a piece of Masonite and place the wrapped board on top of my ironing board. This surface is smooth and firm and can be easily laundered. Iron out any wrinkles on the ironing surface before you begin. Arrange the heat-transfer image upside down on top of the broadcloth so that the image of the heat transfer faces the fabric and the fabric, extends equally beyond all sides of the heat-transfer image.

Pieced heat-transfer image, broadcloth, Wonder Under, and canvas, cut and ready to assemble next to the original photograph.

a) Iron on the back of the heat-transfer paper to bond the image to the fabric.

b) Turn the piece over and iron the back of the fabric.

c) Pull a corner of the paper away from the fabric to check that the image has completely bonded.

d) Starting at a corner, pull the heat-transfer paper off the cooled fabric in a slow, steady motion.

e) Small white lines will be visible where the sections overlapped, but they will be obscured by stitching.

For the Dharma Trading Company heat-transfer paper, use an iron heat setting between "wool" and the lower end of "cotton." Check the product information for the heat-transfer paper you use and keep in mind that heat settings on irons vary. Drain the iron of all water and turn off the steam setting. To begin, iron the center and overlapping seams of the paper. When the transfer has partially bonded all over, remove the tape and go over it with more heat and pressure. Keep moving the iron so that the steam holes don't form a pattern on the fabric. Turn over the fabric/heat-transfer paper stack so that the fabric layer is on top and continue to iron until the fabric is uniformly dark with the image. Make sure the areas around the overlapping paper seams are completely bonded.

Gently pull a corner of the heat-transfer paper away from the fabric to make sure that the image has completely bonded to the fabric. If not, iron the piece some more. Let the fabric cool, then, beginning at the center of the image where the separate sheets of paper meet, pull away the paper one sheet at a time. Pull the paper slowly and smoothly, looking closely for flaky or bubbled areas that may not be fully attached. If you notice such an area, replace the paper and iron again. Make sure the image has cooled before peeling off the paper or the image may re-adhere to the paper instead of the fabric.

As you peel, take care to minimize the amount of image that flakes off at the paper overlaps. A little flaking is inevitable and will appear as thin white lines at the section boundaries. These will be obscured by stitches. You could probably reduce these lines by butting up the sections next to each other instead of overlapping them. If none of the heat-transfer surface will show in the end, this extra effort is not worth the time.

Step 5. The next step is to bond the canvas to the printed broadcloth. There are several bonding products on the market, but I prefer Wonder Under because it includes a backing paper that is useful for several steps of this process.

Check to see that the canvas is still smaller than the image that is now on the broadcloth. During the heat-transfer process the image shrinks slightly, so the canvas may require a little more trimming. If the canvas is not smaller than the image, there could be a white edge around the image after the bonding process. If this happens, cover it with paint or colored permanent marker.

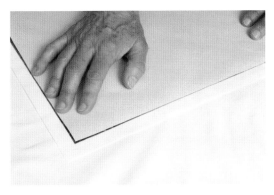

f) Cut the canvas slightly smaller than the image.

g) Separate the Wonder Under web layer from the backing paper.

h) Place the backing paper on the bottom, followed by the broadcloth (printed side down), then place the Wonder Under web on top.

i) Arrange the canvas on top of the Wonder Under.

j) Iron, but do not go beyond the edges of the canvas.

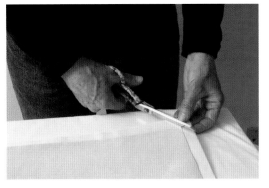

k) Cut off the Wonder Under and broadcloth corners at 45-degree angles.

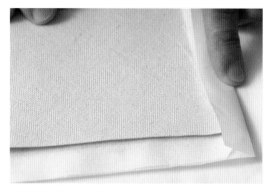

l) Fold the Wonder Under, broadcloth, and backing paper over the canvas to form a hem.

n) Turn the piece over and iron on top of the Wonder Under backing paper.

m) Carefully iron the hem in place.

o) When cool, peel off the backing paper.

Separate the backing and web layers of the Wonder Under and place the backing paper on the ironing surface. Lay the printed broadcloth facedown on the backing paper, then carefully place the web layer on top of the broadcloth, making sure these are aligned with each other. Lay the canvas on top and align it within the boundaries of the image.

Step 6. Use the iron to apply heat to the canvas without hitting the border of Wonder Under around it. The Wonder Under web will melt onto the iron if the iron touches it. Cut off the corners of the Wonder Under and broadcloth at 45-degree angles, cutting next to the corners of the canvas so that there will be no bulk when the edges are turned into a hem.

Use the edge of the backing paper along with the border of fabric and Wonder Under to fold the layers over the canvas as tightly as possible, one side at a time. Use an iron to bond the folded hem in place.

Step 7. Turn the piece over and iron on top of the backing paper to ensure that the broadcloth image is fully bonded to the canvas. Do not iron too long or the Wonder Under will melt into the canvas and no longer hold the two fabrics together. Let the pieces cool, then peel away the backing paper.

The Stitching Process

Examine the transferred image to see whether any details need clarification. Because it can be difficult to discern shape edges while stitching, draw in difficult outlines with a fine-tipped permanent marker. At this point, I make sure that lines that should be straight actually are straight. Sometimes straight lines will curve in a photograph. Although this may not be apparent in a small snapshot, it can become exaggerated in an enlargement or in a different medium. To correct the curved lines caused by the

p) Use a fine-tipped marker to clarify the image.

q) Above: Straighten out curved lines that you want to appear straight—in this case, the boundary between the wall and the window frame.

r) Below: Draw parallel lines across the image to denote the stitching direction.

wide-angle perspective of my camera, I redrew the edge of the window as well as other verticals in the image. (To draw against a dark area, use a white Prismacolor pencil and erase the marks after an initial layer of stitches so that pigment particles from the pencil will not stain or travel up through the layers of thread to the finished surface.) Additional corrections may be necessary during the course of stitching, but this will give you a good start.

I may have made a general plan to stitch vertically, but now I study the shapes more closely to see whether I should tweak the angle slightly to the left or right to make it easier to fill in shapes. Stitching at a slight angle to the edge of a shape works better than using parallel or perpendicular stitches. Once you've decided on a stitching direction, use white or gray Prismacolor pencils to draw parallel lines

s) To prevent unstitched ruffles along the edges, thinly stitch the edges in a more angled direction than the planned final stitch direction.

t) Using thread colors that match the colors of the original photograph, stitch a thin layer across the entire image.

about 1½" to 2" (4 to 5 cm) apart. Although these lines can become confused with vertical elements in the image or with corrections already made to vertical lines, the distinctions will become clear as the stitching progresses.

If you have chosen a vertical or near-vertical stitch direction, work an initial thin layer of angled stitches along the edges. These stitches, which will be mostly covered by subsequent layers of stitching, will help prevent ruffles from forming along the edges where the stitching is not as dense.

The colors and values in a heat-transfer image are slightly different than those in the original photograph, even if that photograph was printed with the same ink-jet printer. To help capture

the true colors, tape the photograph to your sewing machine for reference. You may also want to keep additional photos handy for shape or color details. Begin by stitching a thin layer over the entire image, matching the colors of the original photograph. This first layer introduces you to the colors and mood of the piece and establishes the stitch direction. Don't go too heavy on this first layer—leave room for adding lots of different colors as you develop the surface.

If there are large areas of a single color, try threading the needle with two threads to cover the surface more quickly. You do not need a special needle; just use the two threads as if they were one. However, you must stitch more carefully and more slowly with two threads because there is more drag on the eye of the needle. Using two threads at once in

For quicker progress, let the thread temporarily float between shapes stitched with the same color.

the top means that less thread is used on the back, allowing more thread to be added to the surface. This is particularly helpful in dark areas where it is difficult to get the color and texture rich enough and deep enough to absorb light. If you do use two threads in one needle, route the threads on opposite sides of the tension disk.

If several shapes will be stitched with the same color, stitch several areas before clipping them, allowing the thread to cross over other areas. Sometimes I do this all over the piece in several colors and wait until I am watching TV to clip the floats.

You will have fewer thread ends popping to the front if you clip the threads on the front first. Turn the piece over and gently tug on the bobbin thread to pull the top-thread end through the fabric. Then

clip the bobbin thread. If the floats are short, don't cut the bobbin thread at all. Although some ends will work their way to the surface, this technique will keep them to a minimum. When you work in a small area where a loose end would be distracting or change a detail, lock the ends of the threads by stitching up and down in the same spot a few times.

The goal at this stage is to stitch most of the entire surface, although it is fine to leave small areas unstitched until later. I make mental notes about where there is likely to be more or less constriction in the fabric and which areas may expand more than other areas. If some areas expand or contract more than others, the piece will not lie flat when it is finished (see the sections on patches and darts on pages 68 and 69).

Bright greens, blue, and purple add visual excitement to the turquoise-painted wood.

After the initial layer is in place, erase as many of the Prismacolor lines as possible, but don't be surprised if some pigment remains caught in the tooth of the fabric. Use a gentle touch when erasing to prevent damaging or removing the heat transfer from the canvas. Small bare spots can be easily covered with more stitching, but you may lose crucial details if large patches come off.

Now is a good time to add thin layers of more extreme colors. Adding more subtle colors over the top of these will allow them to offer bits of visual excitement without being as blatant as they seem now.

The next step is to bring small areas to near completion, one at a time. These may be refined closer to the completion of the piece. Choose a section that can be completed in a day (for me, about a 20" to 45" [51 to 115 cm] square, depending on the complexity). Begin with easier parts and progress to more difficult areas as you become in tune with the piece. Focus on isolated areas and try not to become distracted by the rest of the piece. Consider the surrounding sections only if you have stitched so heavily that puckers form in adjacent unstitched areas. If this happens, you must stitch just enough in these areas to ease the puckering, or it may be difficult to stitch evenly among the puckers, the next day. In this piece, I began in the central area with the plant, pot, and floor because I was concerned that this area might bulge if I stitched the wood textures beside it first. I knew that the long vertical areas of the wood could easily constrict more than the central plant image; by completing the plant area first, I felt I would be more able to keep the wood area under control.

With realism, it is important to decide how pronounced the details should be. Textures or colors that are too sharp may destroy the desired sense of illusion. On the other hand, a piece can lack conviction if there is not enough definition. Teaching yourself and practicing the art of careful observation are the first steps in developing skills of representation; learning how to create subtle differences is the next. Taking the time to add one more layer of thread or just a few stitches to make a color or line less obvious may make the difference between an "in your face" effect and one that gracefully blends with the image. Think of your work process as disciplined obsession.

If color relationships are of great importance (as in realism), avoid using outlines to separate shapes unless that is a conscious style choice. Instead, delineate shapes with value differences as for the image of scissors on page 66. Outlines work like fences—they hold colors within bounds

A detail of the plant, pot, and floor area is shown in this semi-finished detail.

as though they were cattle and make it hard for adjacent colors to interact. Just as it is difficult to climb a fence, it is difficult for the eye to travel across lines. That is not to say that lines and linear elements are not important. Because the eye is more likely to travel along lines, use subtle linear elements to the draw the eye from one place to another.

While working within each small area, study the nuances of color, value, and shape. I like to think of myself as the thing being depicted—I "become" the leaf or the peeling paint. Study things closely to understand them in a way that casually moving through your environment would never allow. The opportunity to observe details and color is a gift to yourself.

Gradually stitch and expand out from the area where you started, evaluating your progress as you go. Pin your work to a wall (or a sheet of foam board) and view it from a distance. Make your artwork worth looking at—aim for it to look both effortless and amazing.

When the stitching is complete, steam-press the piece from the back. You may need to get it fairly wet and pull on it in the direction that is already stretching to flatten it completely. Finally, use acrylic paint to touch up any bare spots on the edges, matching the thread colors as closely as possible.

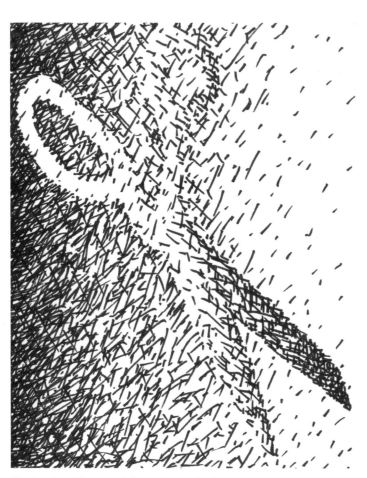

Simple value differences define an image of scissors.

Oppostite: *Window with Aloe*, Carol Shinn 2008, 17" x 13" (43 x 33 cm). Machine stitching on fabric. Photographer: Randall Shinn. Collection of the artist.

Troubleshooting

Sometimes you'll see that an area isn't working out as well technically as you'd like. Rather than give up on the entire piece, try fixing or improving the problem area.

Changing a Color

If a color isn't working, change it. When it isn't dark enough, brush on a darker shade of paint. Thinned acrylic can dull the surface, but fabric paint is more transparent and may not cover the mistake as well. In either case, stitch over the painted surface to make it blend with the rest of the piece. If the original color is too dark, it is better to rip out the problem and restitch the area.

Defining a Straight Edge

If you have trouble defining the straight edge on a shape, temporarily lay a strip of masking tape along the edge, then carefully stitch right up to the edge of the tape. The tape provides a visual guide that is cleaner than a drawn line because a drawn line will bump over the threads, get messy, and be hard to cover. This technique works best on a surface that already has some stitching—masking tape placed directly on a heat transfer may remove part of the transfer when it is pulled off.

Ripping Out

Ultimately, the stitching should look effortless. If an isolated area looks over-labored or clumsy, you have two choices: rip out the stitches and rework the area or cut out the area altogether and replace it with a patch of new stitching. Ripping out and restitching is the first choice. This may happen several times on each piece. I use magnifying headgear when I use a ripping tool so that I can see what I am doing. The aim is to get the thread out without ripping out bits of the base fabric as well. I find that a strong T-pin pulls out small stitches more easily than a conventional ripping tool does. Tweezers are useful for pulling out loose bits of thread.

Feather the amount of remaining stitches so that the new stitches will blend into the existing stitches without creating a lump. Trim the remaining thread ends with scissors. If the canvas becomes damaged, reinforce it by bonding a patch of lightweight fabric to the back of the canvas before restitching. You can also use a little thinned acrylic paint to hold down any loose fibers or threads on the front before restitching.

Creating a Patch

Larger areas or those in which the canvas has been damaged will require a patch. First, thin out the stitching around the area that will be taken out. Cutting out the offending area may cause the edge around the hole to ruffle because the fabric will expand and pucker as it is released from stitching. This will be taken care of later with stitching.

Make a patch that is slightly larger than the hole by drawing and painting on a fresh piece of canvas (it should shrink to size with stitching). Work all but the last layer of stitching on the patch, leaving a small unstitched border around the edge where it will be stitched to the main fabric. Make sure that the stitch direction of the patch matches the stitch direction of the piece.

Cut out the stitched patch and paint the edges as well as the edges of the hole. (For more on painting edges, see Making Darts at right.) Using strips of lightweight fabric and Wonder Under, bond the patch you have just stitched to the back of the piece, placing it over the hole you have cut. There may still be ruffles where the patch and the main piece come together. Working lightly at first, layer stitches over the boundary between the patch and the main piece, hatching with different-sized stitch strokes and carefully matching colors and stitch directions. Gradually the puckers should subside. If a lump begins to form where the fabric edges come together, try to put the needle (with thread) through the fabric in the middle of the lump as you stitch over it. Try not to make an even line with the punctures or stitches as you do this. By bringing the needle down in the middle of the lump, you will push it downward as well as break the pattern of previous stitches that have hopped over the lump.

It may seem impossible at first, but with perseverance you can disguise nearly anything. I once had a commission for a very large piece that wasn't working out to be the right size. The image had become terribly distorted and the proportions were all wrong; it was the stuff of nightmares. I cut the piece into nine separate parts, added stitched fabric between them, and was able to resolve the piece and even deliver it on time!

Making Darts

When I first finished *Window with Aloe*, I could see that the center bulged, despite my efforts to control the contraction of the vertical stitching on the wood imagery. I eliminated the bulge by cutting a slit through the focal point of the aloe leaves and overlapping the two edges to form a dart.

If you find that a dart is necessary, first analyze the problem to determine the best place to cut. A dart is easiest to disguise in a "busy" area because the viewer's eye will focus on the image instead of irregularities in the surface. It also will be easier to disguise if the cut is made along a wavy or jagged line that goes across the direction of stitching, rather than in the same direction. This allows you to more easily hatch the new stitching into the existing embroidery and cover cut edges that might fray.

Begin by making a short cut. Overlap the two sides to see whether the cut is enough to flatten the area. If not, continue cutting a little at a time, angling each cut to form a jagged line. The area should lie flat once the overall cut is long enough. The overlapping part will be cut out. In *Window with Aloe*, the two sides of the cut overlapped by almost ¼" (6 mm).

When making a dart, use masking tape to delineate the edge of the first cut made.

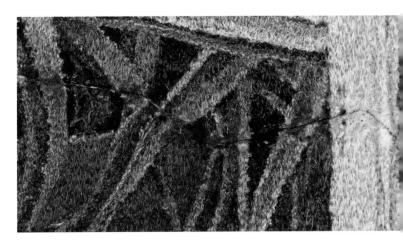

Paint the cut edges of the dart.

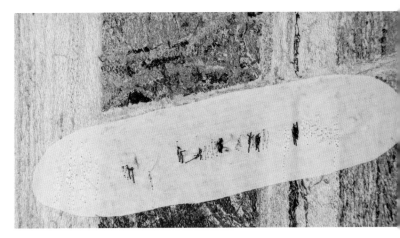

Bond a patch to the underside of the cut (shown here after stitching was begun).

The finished mended area.

Place masking tape next to the jagged cut. When you lift the top edge of the jagged cut, the masking tape will show you how much the two sides overlapped. Cut out and discard the extra fabric of the bulge by cutting along the line formed by the edge of the masking tape. The two edges of the dart should fit flush with each other like pieces of a puzzle.

Next, carefully rip out some of the stitching along the edges of the dart and pull as many of the loose ends to the back as possible by clipping the front thread first, then pulling on the loose ends of the bobbin threads with tweezers. Paint the cut edges with acrylic paint diluted to the consistency of cream to reduce fraying and to cover the white fabric base. Make a patch of lightweight fabric and Wonder Under and bond it over the cut on the underside of the piece.

Begin stitching across the cut, working briefly here and there before gradually mending and hiding the cut completely. If a ridge begins to develop along the seam, carefully aim the needle into the top of the ridge at least part of the time as you stitch. Use a pin or the tip of your scissors to push down on the ridge as you stitch. Take care not to over-stitch the area or you'll create a new buckle.

Presenting and/or Framing an Embroidery

Determining the best way to present your work is crucial. If you present your work haphazardly, or if you make poor framing choices, the quality of your work will suffer. Small two-dimensional pieces usually look best framed or mounted onto some type of background. There are always exceptions, but most small textiles look vulnerable, unfinished, or insignificant without some kind of definition that separates them from the wall. Embroidery should be presented so that it is clear that the piece is a textile and not another art medium. If a mat is used to cover the edges of a piece, the mat will be more appropriate if it's covered with fabric than if is cut from mat board. If the edges of you artwork are presentable, you can mount it against a fabric-covered background so that the edges are exposed. This is the way I mount my embroideries.

Using regular-weight sewing thread, I handstitch my embroidery near its edges to archival foam board. I match the handsewing thread to the colors of the piece. I then hand tack the foam board with the embroidery to a fabric-covered background foam board with heavy sewing thread. I always choose a black background to make the colors pop.

Opinions differ as to whether an embroidery should be placed behind glass or Plexiglas or shown without either. Good UV-light protection will certainly increase the life of any textile. Museum glass, which offers both UV protection and a nonglare surface, is the best, but it can be expensive and make it difficult to pack a piece for shipping—many shipping companies are rough on packages and will not insure anything that is breakable, even if double boxed. If you plan to ship your artwork, Plexiglas may be a better choice. It is also available with UV protection. Be aware that Plexiglas scratches easily (and may need to be replaced after each shipment) and creates static electricity that attracts bits of lint. Whichever material you choose, make sure the frame is deep enough so that the artwork doesn't touch the glass or Plexiglas—direct contact can lead to moisture condensation, mildew, and other problems.

I now mount my embroideries without glass or Plexiglas. Consequently, my pieces are unprotected and vulnerable to dirt, friction, light, and insects, but I believe that these dangers are offset by the benefit of viewers being able to see my work more clearly. The frames I use are 2" (5 cm) deep and come with a matching spacer to accommodate glass or Plexiglas if a buyer so chooses. To ship a piece, I cover the front with plastic wrap and pack it in a double box.

A frame may be inappropriate for a large or sculptural piece. For such a piece, caution buyers and exhibition managers about potential damage caused by light or greasy fingers and be specific with your display instructions. *The Care and Preservation of Textiles* (see Recommended Books on page 172) has excellent guidance and diagrams for attaching linings to large flat textiles, as well as methods for hanging and storing them. There are also many websites on the basics of quilt care.

Chapter Four:
Adding Variety

"Textiles are about every sensibility; the emotional content is the textile, the sense of touching and feeling and seeing." —Alice Kettle, contemporary British artist

Adding variety and complexity to your embroideries can be a way to engage your audience, particularly as they come closer to your work. Use careful judgment in integrating variety so that it supports the overall visual effect—too many techniques or overdone textures can spoil a piece. Experiment with techniques from this chapter, or of your own invention, to develop new ideas and skills. What follows are works from other artists and examples of my own experimentation.

Thread Choice and Purposeful Communication

Art is a form of communication. Before you decide on which materials to use for a piece (including thread), consider what you wish to communicate. When is it important for the materials to seem to disappear so that the viewer considers just the image or design? How much should the process or the various materials be apparent? There has been a long debate in all the arts over "the cunning or flamboyant" versus "the plain and direct." Decide how theatrical you want to make your piece.

Calliope, Alice Kettle 2006, 21¾" x 12¾" (55 x 32 cm). Machine stitching on fabric. Photographer: James Newell. Collection of Rebecca Morgan.

For an illusion of reality, for example, you might choose to have techniques and materials show less, so that the image is of foremost importance. To focus attention on the composition, use threads that are similar in appearance, rather than mixing thick and thin or dull and shiny so that the stitches will seem to disappear into the image. On the other hand, you might choose to develop a personal style of "mark making" that emphasizes the embroidery process, or you might choose a subject that would be more effectively communicated by overtly displaying the materials and the stitches used. If, for example, your goal is to comment on the history of design or the traditions of textiles, it may be appropriate to use decorative stitches, threads, and materials.

Stitch Possibilities

There are many ways to apply stitches in freestyle machine embroidery. Consider how stitch direction, density, type, and tension can be used to your advantage.

Straight Stitches

You can get a variety of effects with just the straight stitch setting on your machine. Multidirectional stitches can create a sense of motion and energy.

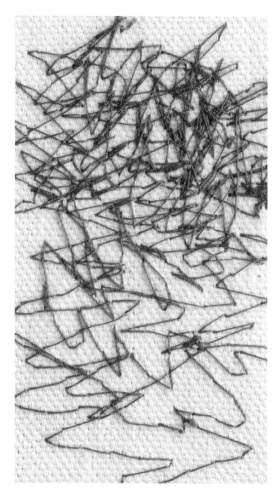

Move the fabric at different angles with each stroke to create a sense of energy.

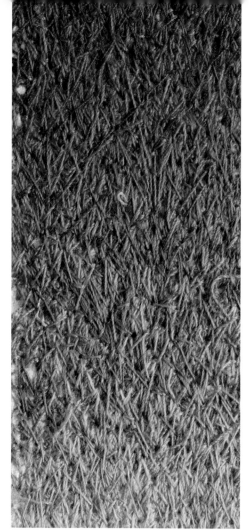

Layer multidirectional stitching to add texture to a hue gradation.

Instead of moving the fabric back in forth in parallel strokes—or lines of motion—change the angle of the fabric with each pass, sometimes stitching on the right bias, sometimes on the left, and sometimes along the grain of the fabric. This type of stitching keeps image distortion to a minimum and is an effective way to create shading and color gradations.

Stitch in a variety of angles, but instead of changing directions continuously, form small groups of parallel stitches that go first one way and then another. To save time, stitch several clumps of one color before clipping the connecting threads. Experiment with a gradual shift from a continuous mix of stitch directions to small distinct clumps or crystal shapes.

Opposite Above: Use a light application of stitches to allow the base fabric to show. Here, each layer of stitches was made in a different direction.

Opposite Below: Form a texture gradation by gradually shifting from a continuous mix of stitch directions (left) to distinct groups of stitches (right).

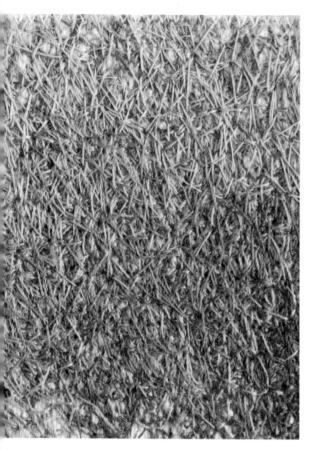

Circular stitching forms granite stitch. Move the fabric in large circles to create a sense of energy.

Move the fabric in small circles to create a sense of control.

Instead of moving the fabric back and forth in parallel strokes, move it in circles to form a **granite stitch**. It takes practice to make your circles round instead of angular—to make smoother circles, run the machine faster in relation to your hand movement so that the individual stitches are smaller. In general, larger circles will appear more energetic and smaller circles will appear smoother and more controlled.

Wiggling, meandering stitches (**vermicelli stitch**) can create an interesting fill, especially when contrasted with other textures. Other stitches also can be made into fill patterns. Sondra Dorn used stitched handwriting to provide content as well as texture in *Shielded Space: Orange and Blue* (see page 79).

Opposite: Use vermicelli stitch as an interesting fill pattern.

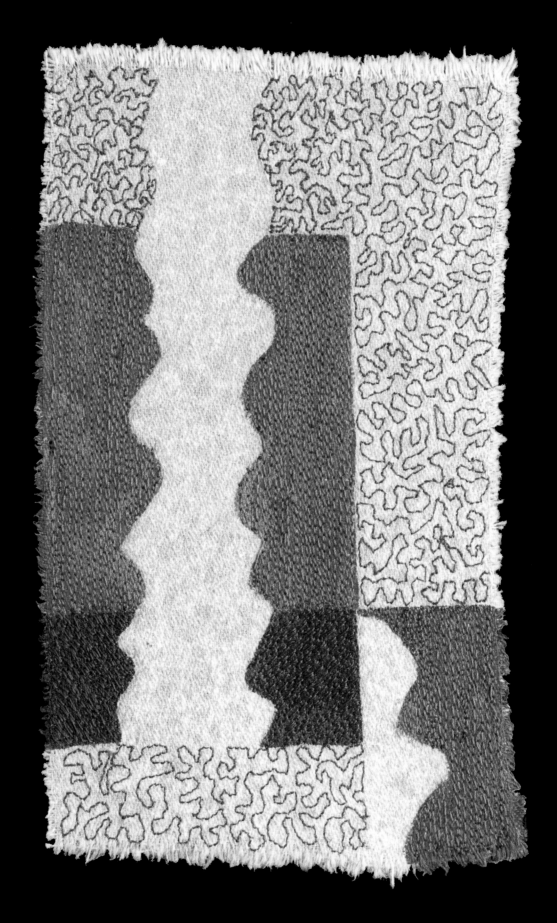

Detail of *Shielded Space: Orange and Blue.*

Shielded Space: Orange and Blue, Sondra Dorn 2000,
30" x 30" (76 x 76 cm). Fabric collage and thread.
Photographer: Tim Barnwell. Collection of the artist.

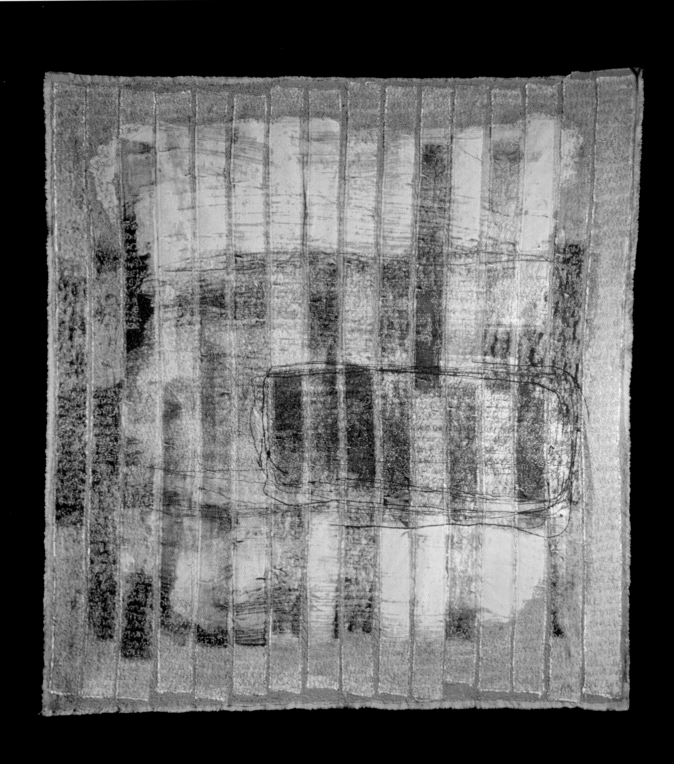

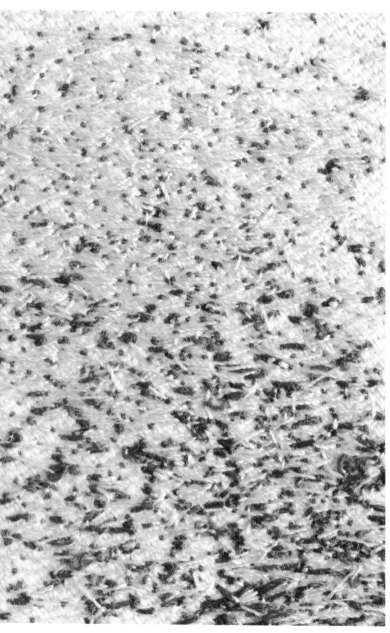

Loosen the bobbin tension in relation to the top tension to allow bits of the bobbin thread to show on the surface.

By altering the bobbin tension, you can make small dots of bobbin thread come to the surface (**color spotting**). More extreme versions of altered tension can produce bobbin dashes (**whipstitch**) and full loops (**feather stitching**). Alice Kettle's *Calliope* (see page 72) shows the rich textures that can be created by changes in thread tension. Kettle has developed these into a unique style of mark making.

To alter bobbin tension, first tighten the top thread (move the dial on the front of your machine to a higher number). You will probably also need to loosen the bobbin tension (turn the bobbin screw to the left a little at a time), but make a note of the starting angle of the screw crevice so you'll be able to return to it later. It works well to draw this on masking tape and attach it to your machine so that you don't lose it. Some machine dealers recommend purchasing a second bobbin case so that one can be used for ordinary sewing and the other can be used for freestyle embroidery. This is a particularly good idea if you own a machine with a horizontal bobbin race, which can be more temperamental than a vertical bobbin case. If you have put the thread through the hole in the bobbin case finger, take it out; this will help loosen the bobbin thread. Adjust the top and bottom tensions in small increments— if the tensions of either the top or the bobbin are too extreme, the machine may jam. Try a variegated thread in the bobbin; it will make a wonderful variation in the dots.

For the bobbin thread to show best:

- The top thread should contrast sharply with the bobbin thread.
- The lines of stitches should be short and change directions abruptly.
- The machine speed should be a bit slower than usual in relation to your hand movements.
- The layers of paint or previous stitches should be kept thin where you plan to use this technique.
- Select stitches that naturally tend to pull up the bobbin thread, such as curved lines and zigzag stitches.

Moss stitch forms a loopy surface of thread. To begin, create areas of bobbin texture using whipstitch or feather stitch. Bond fabric to the back of your embroidery with Wonder Under or a similar product to secure the bobbin thread, then carefully rip out the top thread. Alternately, use a dissolvable top thread that will rinse away with water. For a similar effect, try a clear nylon thread on the top (but be aware that nylon thread can melt when ironed at a high heat setting). In general, clear nylon thread will be a bit more visible if used against dark backgrounds than light backgrounds.

Theoretically, you could keep loosening the bobbin until loops form on the top surface of the fabric. However, at a certain point, the top thread will become too tight and will pull on the fabric, the stitches will skip, or the machine will jam up with stitches caught in the hook. It is more effective to work upside down, because it is easier to make the top threads form loops on the underside of the fabric (see page 82).

To work upside down, first loosen the top tension, then tighten the bobbin tension and put the bobbin thread through the finger hole of the bobbin case, if there is one. From there it's a matter of trial and error—experiment to see what happens. If the thread creates too much of a loopy wad or if thread catches in the hook, the tension difference between the top and the bobbin threads is too great. Make small adjustments until you get the effect you want. Depending on the type of thread you used, cut out or dissolve the thread as described for moss stitch or leave the bobbin thread in place.

You may also want to work upside down if you are using weak or textured metallic threads. Although large-eye needles are available for metallics, you still may have problems with thread breakage because of the strain put on it by the tension disks. Put the decorative thread in the bobbin and a plain thread in the needle. Turn your fabric over and stitch on the underside.

To create moss stitch, pull out the top thread after using whipstitch or feather stitch, or use a dissolvable thread in the top (top) and rinse after stitching (bottom).

Create large loops by working upside down with a loose top tension so that the top thread forms loops on the underside.

When you work upside down, you will not be able to see the front of the fabric to guide your stitching. Previous stitching may help guide you, but if you're not sure where to stitch, outline your shapes with straight stitches before beginning. The bobbin side of these outlines will provide a guide for the rest of the stitching. Alternately, use pins to mark the area where you want to stitch. Turn the fabric over and draw connecting lines between the pins. Then remove the pins and stitch (shown opposite).

Lower Left: When working upside down, mark the area to be stitched with straight pins.

Above Left: Draw connecting lines between the pins on the underside.

Below: Here, the accent lines were made with a heavy metallic thread. Additional rust-colored moss stitch fills part of the design.

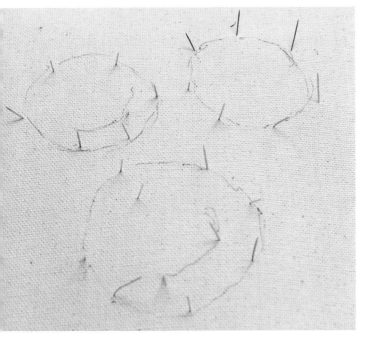

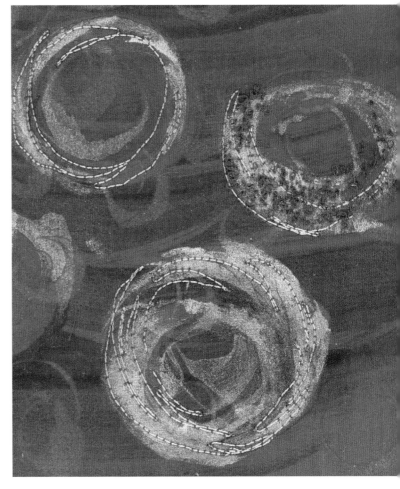

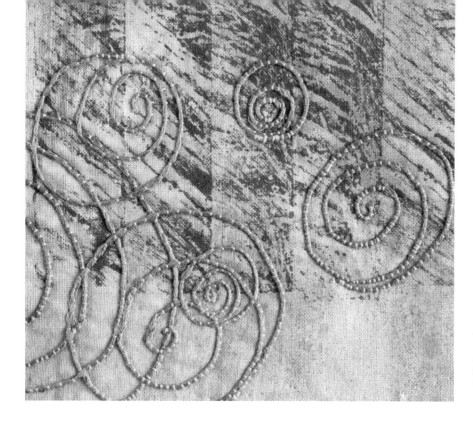

Left: The cable stitch in this sample was made with six strands of hand-embroidery floss.

Below: In this example, heavy pearl cotton was used in the bobbin without tension—note the quirky loops and curls.

You can use heavy threads, several strands of embroidery floss, or smooth yarn if you wind them by hand onto the bobbin and work with the fabric upside down. The top thread usually shows and gives the effect of hand couching over the heavier fibers. Be sure not to loosen it so far that the tension spring (the little piece of metal attached to the bobbin case with a screw) moves out of place when you try to pull the yarn under it.

If the bobbin thread or yarn breaks when you sew, try removing it from the bobbin tensioning spring. Put it through the hole adjacent to the spring, if there is one. Some machines equipped with vertical bobbin races have closed bobbin cases without a hole next to the bobbin spring and therefore are limited to threads that can pass through the bobbin-tensioning spring. You may bypass the spring without going through any hole in the bobbin case on some machines with horizontal bobbin races. If you have a horizontal race or drop-in bobbin machine, it is worth experimenting with heavier threads. Work slowly and be prepared for the quirky loops and curls that result from the lack of tension.

Zigzag- and Satin-Stitch Effects

The zigzag setting is extremely versatile. Check to make sure that your zigzag width fits within the confines of the darning foot. Move the machine wheel slowly by hand first to make sure that the needle doesn't hit the foot. Zigzag stitches set very close together (as for working a buttonhole) make a **satin stitch**. This stitch is ideal for defining formal linear shapes. You'll get the most even stitches if you use a regular presser foot and work with the feed dogs up.

Zigzag and satin stitch are ideal for attaching and outlining **appliqués** (applied fabric shapes). Small zigzag dots (**bead stitches**) can also be used to attach appliqué shapes as well as other elements. To bead-stitch with a darning foot and without the feed dogs engaged, make several zigzag stitches over each other without moving the fabric. To bead-stitch with a regular foot and the feed dogs engaged, use a stitch length of zero. When working without any foot, as I did for the sample using the prickly pear skeleton on page 86, hold down the item close to where the needle enters the fabric. Watch your fingers, and don't forget to lower the lever that usually controls the foot—this engages the thread tension.

To produce **openwork**, use satin stitch to define closed shapes (such as circles or triangles), then cut away the fabric from the center of these shapes as closely as possible without cutting the stitching.

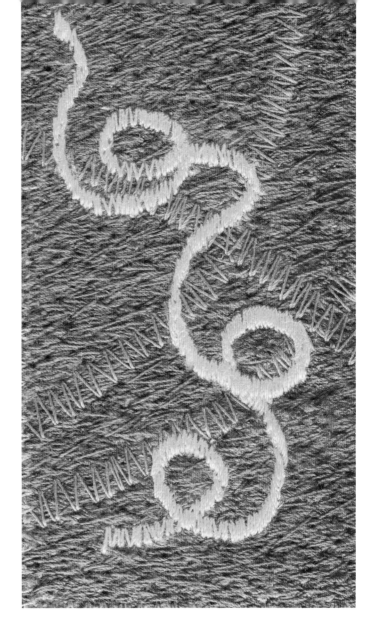

Above Right: Satin stitch (closely spaced zigzag) can be used to create linear shapes. Use a regular foot and stitch with the feed dogs up.

Right: Gradually change the stitch width to make dynamic shapes and lines (see Susan Brandeis's *Succulence* on page 146). Use a regular presser foot, keep the feed dogs up, and make changes to the stitch width when the needle is up.

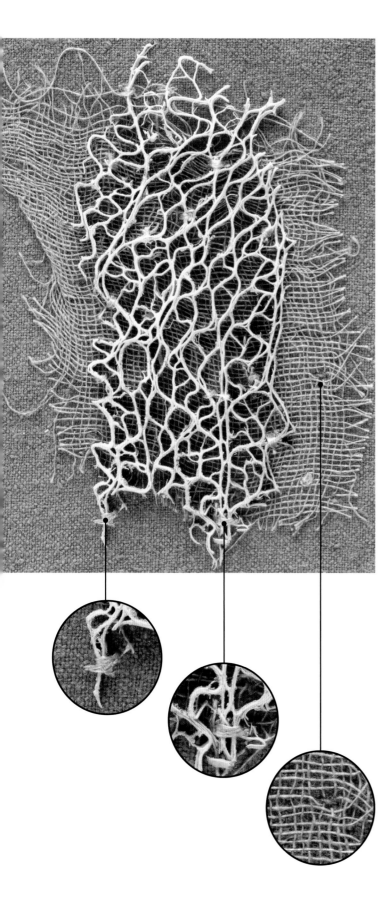

Left: In this sample, I attached the cheesecloth with tiny bead stitches that were almost invisible against the open structure of the weave. To attach the prickly pear skeleton, I removed the presser foot and slowly zigzagged larger bead stitches over the skeleton in several places with thread to match the color of the skeleton.

Below: Use bead stitches for patterns and accents.

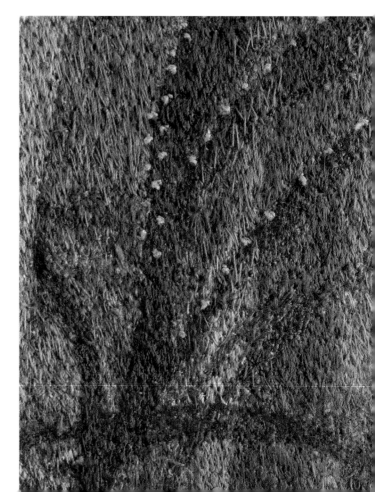

Above: Create daisylike shapes by pivoting the fabric around a single point as you zigzag.

Right: Create small rounded shapes by using a circular motion, keeping the fabric in the same orientation while stitching.

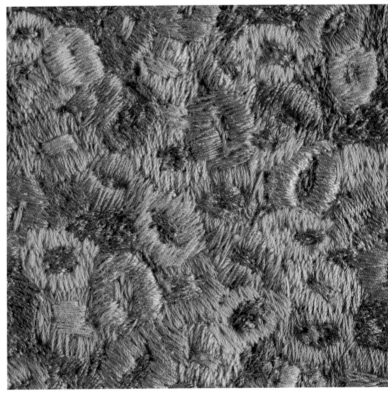

Make a solid fill with even rows of zigzags, changing and layering colors for interest. Put the feed dogs up and use a regular foot.

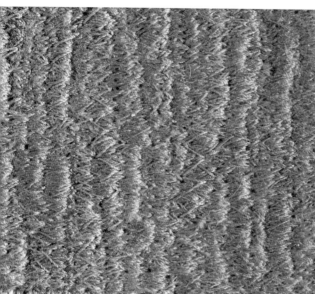

Create a solid fill by varying the width, density, and placement of the zigzag rows. Audrey Walker uses open rows of zigzag as part of a textured fill. See the detail of *Gaze 1* on page 136.

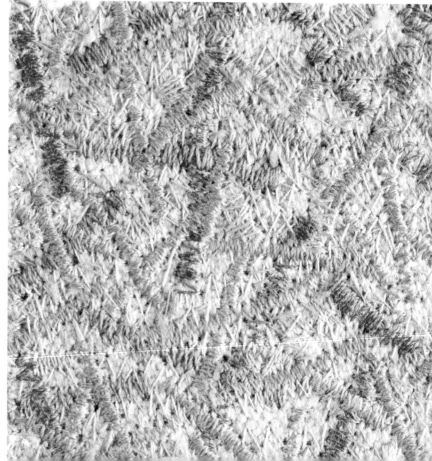

Zigzag bars may be layered in different directions, either using a small stitch length or a longer, more open length. Use a regular foot and put the feed dogs up to keep the rows and stitch length even.

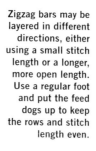

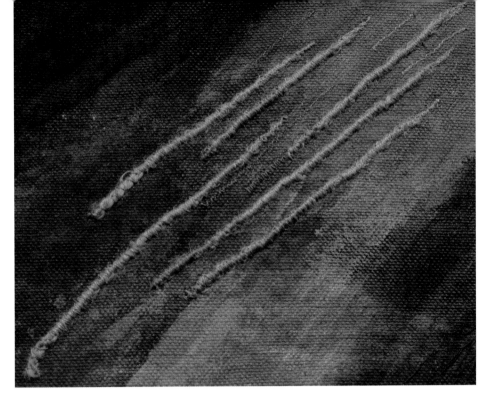

Use satin stitch over thick cords or strands of fibers to create raised bars and ridges.

Narrow strips of knitted fabric are ideal for making cords or raised shapes. As you zigzag over the strip, pull on it gently so it will curl in on itself.

Thick unattached strands also can be zigzagged and used alone or attached to a fabric surface later.

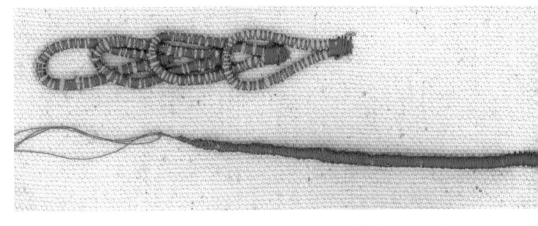

Detail of *Sounds of Nature*. Noriko Narahira used a zigzag
stitch to make cords from twisted strips of printed cotton.

Opposite: *Sounds of Nature*,
Noriko Narahira 1998, 31½"
x 45¼" (180 x 115 cm).
Cotton fabric, thread,
hot-water soluble fabric.
Photographer: Junichi Kanzaki.
Private collection.

Left: In pieces using freestyle straight stitches, zigzag can be useful as a first layer in narrow linear shapes. Closely observe the angle within the zigzag as you stitch (and adjust the angle of the fabric as you stitch) so that the angle within the zigzag matches the angle of your other stitches.

Below: Follow the initial zigzags with freestyle layers to soften the mechanical appearance of the zigzag.

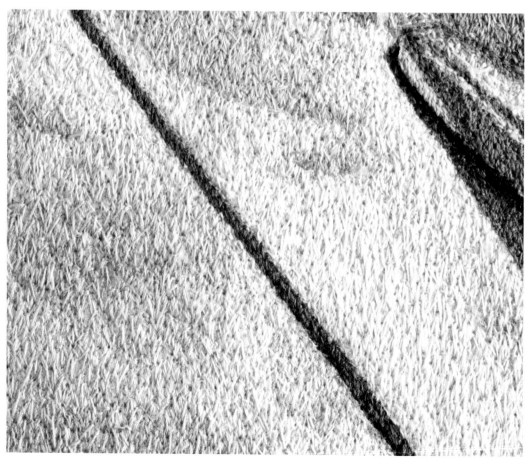

Above: An excellent overall texture can be created using zigzag with a darning foot and with the feed dogs down. Keep changing the angle of the fabric as you stitch and move the fabric around to evenly cover it. Try layering colors or making a color gradation.

Below: Loosen the bobbin tension and tighten the top tension to bring specks of the bobbin thread to the surface.

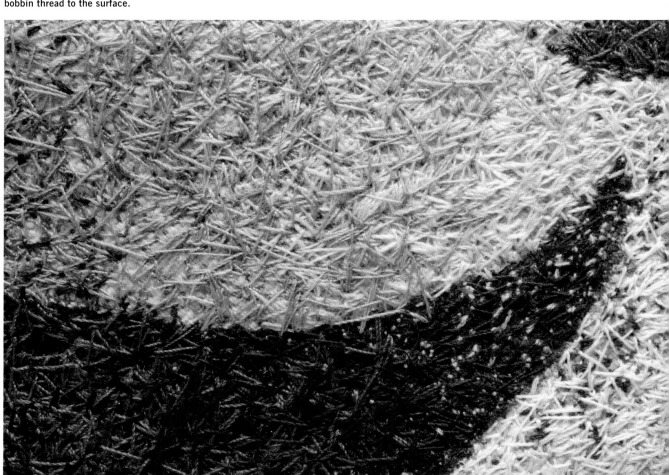

This detail of *Susan Tam* shows how expressive a mixture of zigzag textures and straight stitches can be.

Opposite: *Susan Tam*, Susanne Gregg 2002, 13" x 11" (33 x 28 cm). Machine stitching on fabric. Photographer: Chris Stewart. Collection of Susan Tam.

Above: A short pile texture can be made with satin stitch set on the widest stitch width. Bond another fabric to the back of your piece and run a ripping tool through the center of the zigzags to create the pile. Do this in several layers for a thick pile.

A slightly longer pile can be made using a tailor-tacking foot with the feed dogs up. Use a wide stitch width and a short stitch length. Follow the instructions in your manual for using this foot.

Couching

Couching is an embroidery technique in which one or more threads are laid down on the fabric surface and attached by a finer thread. Both threads are visible. Couching can be used to define linear elements or as part of an overall texture. Loose thread or fibers can be held in place by hand or attached to the surface with fabric glue before stitching. The top stitches can go parallel or across the loose threads or fibers beneath, and there can be a lot of color contrast or very little between the two. The top threads can be stitched with balanced tension, or the bobbin tension can be loosened so that bits of bobbin color show on the surface.

Attaching threads, ribbon, and other materials at intervals allows them to be bunched, looped, or arranged, as I did with the netted onion bags shown opposite. They can be used for their linear design qualities or as an interesting fill.

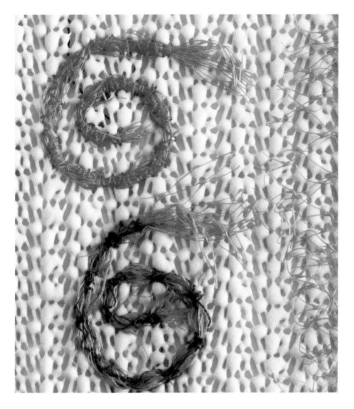

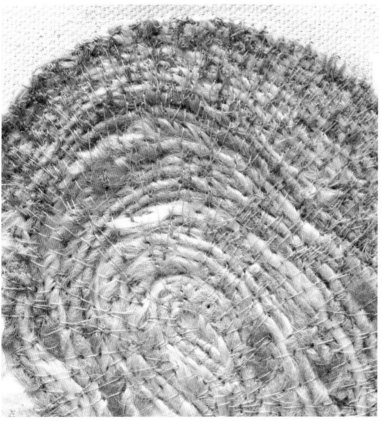

Above Left: Onion bags are couched to rubber matting in this sample.

Above: Couch loose fibers by stitching parallel to the fibers laid down.

Left: In this sample, couching was done across handspun flax that was pressed into the sticky side of a stabilizer called Stabil-Stick Tear-Away (available at quilt shops or Embroidery Online; see Suppliers on page 173). The darker brown bobbin thread was brought up, increasing gradually toward the edge.

Detail of *Perpetua*.
Susan Brandeis laid down many different fibers and
couched them in place with rows of straight stitches.
Appliquéd fern-leaf shapes also helped hold the fibers in
place.

Opposite: *Perpetua*, Susan Brandeis 1998,
47½" × 40" (120.5 x 102 cm). Wool,
alpaca, cotton, dyed threads, felted, dyed,
screen printed, appliquéd, reverse appliquéd, and machine stitched. Photographer: Marc Brandeis. Collection of Atlanta
Gas Light, Atlanta, Georgia.

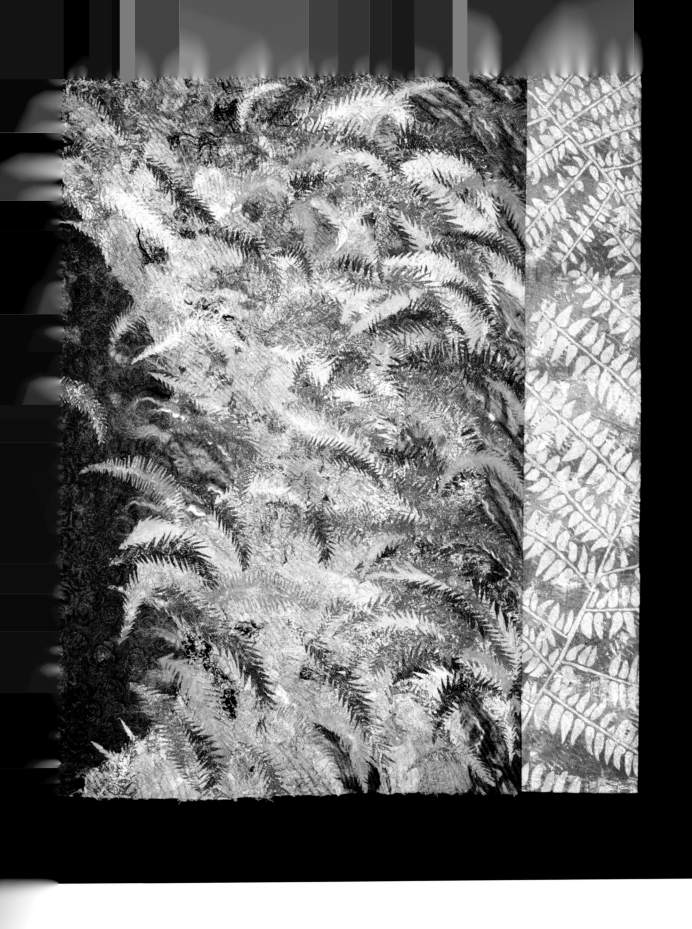

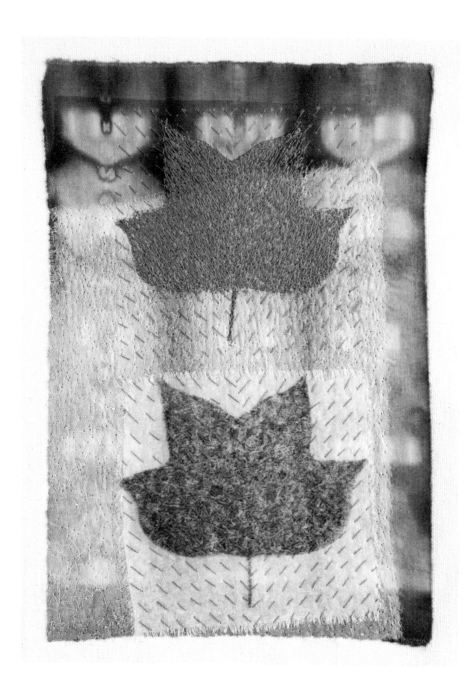

In this example, the textures of the machine-stitched fill in the upper leaf and the looser nylon thread stitching over white silk organza contrast with the formal pattern of red stitches worked by hand.

Machine Stitching Combined with Handstitching

Combining machine and handstitching allows you to have the qualities of both methods of working. Stitches are like syllables and words in a sentence— some seem to disappear in the larger whole and others become points of emphasis. Heavy overstitching can have the same effect as a spoken expletive. In *Dusk* (see page 103), Audrey Walker combines hand and machine stitching, at times making some stitches pronounced and at other times blending them together.

Handstitching here is used both as a focal accent and as
part of the overall texture.

These details of *Dusk* by Audrey Walker show her wonderful understanding of how to blend hand- and machine stitching, allowing each layer of stitches, as well as the fabric, to show.

Opposite: *Dusk*, Audrey Walker 2004, 55" x 19½" (140 x 75 cm). Hand- and machine stitching on fabric. Photographer: Philip Clarke. Collection of the University of Glamorgan.

Attaching Decorative Elements

Beads, stones, and other objects can be added to the surface of an embroidery, but be aware that they draw attention to themselves. Take care to integrate them with the rest of the piece so they don't look like isolated trinkets or afterthoughts. The best embellishments are those that become transformed into something more than themselves. Sometimes a lot of beads or other attachments can create a meaningful texture, whereas just a few can look like insufficient materials or effort on the artist's part. If you want to include embellishments, consider their purpose and relationship to the whole and plan for them from the beginning.

For attaching a series of beads, first string them onto a strong thread or monofilament long enough to allow plenty of space to move the beads back and forth. Stitch a line next to the thread, stitching across the thread before and after each bead as it is moved into place. This should be done without a presser foot, but it can be tricky because each stitch will tend to pull up the fabric and prevent a stitch from forming. Use your fingers to hold the fabric and beads against the plate, close to where the needle enters the fabric. If the fabric is unbacked and lightweight, hold it taut in an embroidery hoop. Attach the hoop so that the fabric lies along the bottom side of the hoop, upside down from the way a hoop is used in hand embroidery.

To attach flat objects such as coins or mirrors, first fasten the object to the fabric with a bit of fabric glue. Remove the presser foot, loosen the bobbin tension to the point of making loops (as described for feather stitch on page 80), and then stitch closely around the object, being very careful not to hit it. The top thread will gather in over the top of the object as the bobbin thread pulls up around the sides to hold it in place.

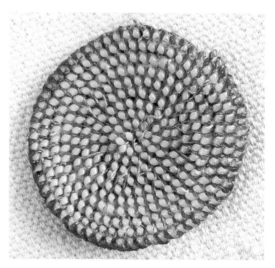

Above: With the presser foot removed, materials such as this coil of nylon zipper teeth can be attached by carefully stitching over them as the machine wheel is turned by hand.

Below: To attach a flat coin, stitch closely around it using loose bobbin tension so that the top thread gathers in over the top and the bobbin thread pulls up around the sides.

To apply beads, string them onto a strong thread or monofilament and stitch across that before and after each bead.

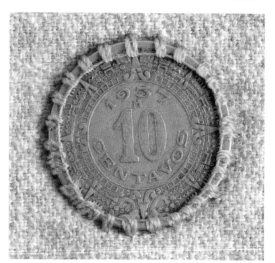

Edge Considerations

The edges that define the perimeter of your artwork are important to the overall success of the piece. Make plans for your edge before you begin on the piece itself. If you don't want the viewer's eye drawn to the edge, use a simple treatment. For an unadorned edge, bond broadcloth to the canvas, then fold the edges to the back side before you begin stitching. If you use canvas with the grain straight, the edge can be torn to leave a small fringe; this can be painted to match after the stitching is complete. For a more defined edge, use satin stitch or decorative stitches. If the fabric is lightweight, fold under a hem and iron it in place. Zigzag along the fold line, then trim away the excess fabric. More elaborate edges can be made for pieces that have a decorative emphasis. Yarn stitched into the edge treatment can help stabilize edges and keep them even.

Experiment. What happens when you zigzag an edge on knitted fabric with no stabilizer beneath? What kinds of lace edges could you stitch using a water-soluble stabilizer? Could another fiber create a unique edge? Marian Bijlenga used horsehair in *Sampler Dots* (see page 107) and left the hair exposed along the edges.

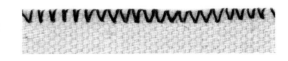

Make a simple but more defined edge in three easy steps.
1. Zigzag with a small stitch length around the edges once or twice before you begin stitching the piece (top).
2. After the piece is complete, paint the edge with thinned acrylic, matching the zigzag color. This stabilizes the edge and will reduce stretching or ruffling.
3. Do a final layer of close zigzag (center). Bits of the canvas can show through if the edges are not painted (bottom).

More elaborate edges can be made for pieces that have a decorative emphasis. Yarn stitched into the edge treatment can help stabilize edges and keep them even. Try combining zigzag with decorative machine-controlled patterns.

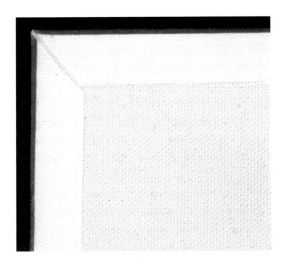

To create a clean edge, bond broadcloth to the canvas and fold over the edges of the broadcloth to the back side before you begin to stitch, seen here from the back.

Wrap the edge with a printed fabric for a contrasting frame.

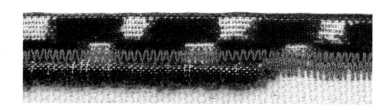

Silk organza and yellow cord wrap over a satin-stitch edge. The fringe faces into the piece and is held in place with a decorative stitch.

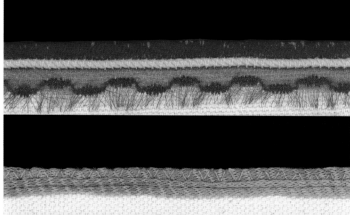

Two rows of multicolored knit tube ribbon.

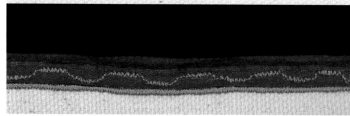

Two layers of satin ribbon are used with decorative and satin stitches.

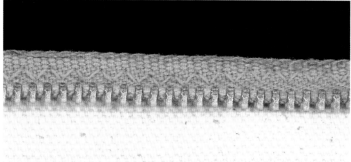

Surprise elements such as zippers can be used in edge treatments.

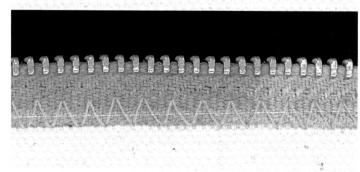

Sampler Dots, Marian Bijlenga 2004, 18" × 18"
(46 x 46 cm). Horsehair, fabric, monofilament.
Photographer: Ron Zijlstra. Private collection.

Variety in Stitchable Surfaces

Experiment with different surfaces to expand new creative directions. If you allow the fabric or other base surface to show under the stitches, this surface will participate in the completed design. As you experiment, ask yourself what one surface offers over others. Ask how each surface could be used to its best advantage.

Paper has great stiffness, but it does not have the tensile strength or stretch of fabric. Stitching must be done lightly or the paper will disintegrate from needle punctures. Use as small a needle as possible and large stitches to minimize the size and frequency of the needle punctures. Paper wears out needles more quickly than cloth does, so discard a needle that has been used to stitch paper.

Stitching on photographs can create interesting effects. The paper's strength is compromised by needle punctures, however, and small white spots appear at each puncture hole. These can appear exaggerated in the context of the image.

In *Quilter's Table*, Anne Eckley used Mod Podge (a combination glue, sealer, and finish for decoupage) to collage a patterned paper bag with wrinkled tissue paper. She layered lightweight interfacing and fabric onto the back with Mod Podge, and then secured the layers by zigzagging around the edges. She then painted the surface with acrylic paint and allowed much of the leathery surface to be exposed around the machine stitching.

Top Left: Needle puncture holes are distinctly visible in the dark areas of a photograph.

Left: Heavy stitching can damage watercolor paper—it caused the corner to tear off in this sample.

Opposite: *Quilter's Table*, Anne Eckley 2006, 12" × 7½" (31 x 19 cm). Paper, fabric, Mod Podge, thread. Photographer: Ann Swanson. Private collection.

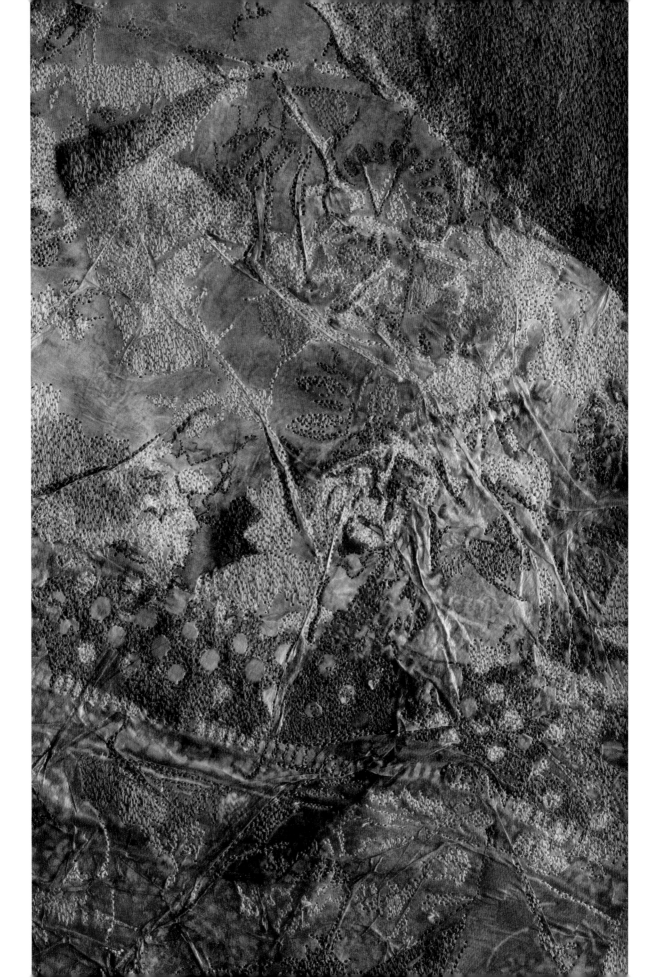

Thin, flexible plastics, leather, and gut can also be lightly stitched, but, like paper, the surface will deteriorate from repeated needle punctures. Special needles are available that reduce damage to leather—these may work well on plastics and similar materials.

Tyvek, a paperlike synthetic material often used in postal envelopes, is difficult to tear and withstands considerable bending and friction. But, like paper, it has no stretch when used as a base material for stitching. Gwen Hedley, in her book *Surfaces for Stitch: Plastics, Films, and Fabric*, mentions that it can be fed through some computer printers. When heated it will shrink and bubble in interesting ways. Be aware that it gives off noxious fumes when heated because it is composed of polyethylene fibers. Heat it only outside and wear a respirator. For more about working with Tyvek and other interesting surfaces, consult *Surfaces for Stitch* (see Recommended Books on page 172).

Craft felt is not stiff enough to stitch on unless it has been bonded to another fabric, but thin industrial felt, which is both strong and stiff, works quite well. Noriko Narahira's *Scenes of White 2* on page 148 is a beautiful example of how industrial felt can be used as a foundation for stitching. Handmade felt can also provide an interesting surface. Pieces of yarn incorporated into the feltmaking process can introduce linear design elements. Such lines, integrated into the felt matrix, provide a good transition to surface additions of wool bobbin stitching and machine- or hand-couched elements.

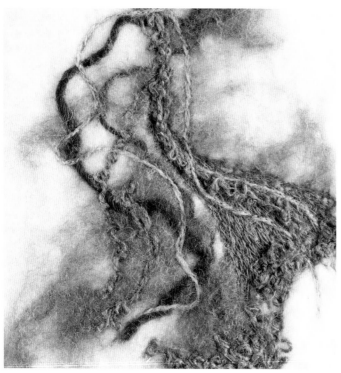

Top Left: Stitching mimics a Polaroid transfer on industrial felt.

Left: Handmade felt provides a strong and interesting surface for stitching.

Leaf shapes were stitched on heavyweight Pellon interfacing, cut out, and added to a sample of the same material.

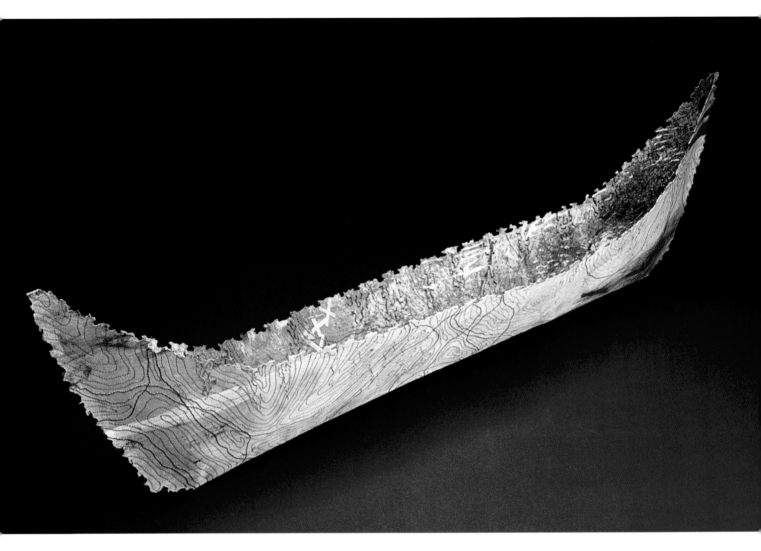

Above: *Red Right Returning #4*, Barbara Lee Smith 2006, 9" x 33" x 4" (23 x 84 x 10 cm). Mixed media, textiles, thread, acrylic on fused and melted synthetic. Photographer: Tom Holt. Collection of the artist.

Right: Detail of *Red Right Returning #4*.

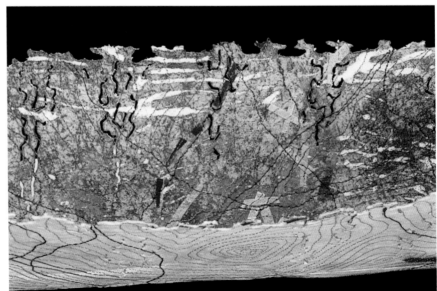

A variety of nonwoven stabilizers are available on the market. They can be drawn on with felt-tipped markers, ironed, and cut without fraying; if stiff or heavyweight, they can take a fair amount of stitching without a hoop. Stabil-Stick Tear-Away has a sticky surface (see the example used with couching on page 97). Peel off the protective backing and attach fabrics, threads, or yarn for stitching. To prevent your needle from gumming up, lightly coat it with a bit of silicone-based lubricant such as Collins Sewer's Aid.

In *Red Right Returning #4*, Barbara Lee Smith used an industrial-weight nonwoven stabilizer, which allowed her the freedom not only to attach elements to the piece but also to cut and burn edges and holes with a soldering iron. To protect yourself from noxious fumes, wear a respirator and work outside when burning synthetic stabilizers.

Pile surfaces can make good visual contrasts with either hand- or machine stitching. Try stitching on velvet (see *Voluptuous Velvet* by Jean Littlejohn in Recommended Books on page 172). Experiment with as many different kinds of fabrics as you can find—lightweight silks, cheesecloth, netting, knits, worn and used fabrics, high-tech fabrics, upholstery fabrics, and handwovens. Instead of focusing on imagery, I chose a torn washcloth to study texture. I stitched the central square in a gradation of densities, stitching more heavily on the left side than the right.

Above: To see if I could integrate machine stitching with handwoven fabric, I tried cable stitching on a handwoven satin-weave fabric with a painted warp.

Below: The stitching in this sample is used as texture in combination with the pile structure of a washcloth.

Myth Riders, Sara Rockinger 2006, installation of nine panels, each 75" × 43" (191 × 109 cm). Silk gauze and thread. Photographer: Joe Mendoza, CSU Photo Services. Collection of the artist.

Sara Rockinger utilizes the transparency of silk in her overlapping nine-panel installation, *Myth Riders* (see above). The large scale of her work allows viewers to walk around and between these layers. The line drawings seen on and through the silk each suggest the movement of horse and rider and their passage into the distance. The scale of the work made it impractical for her to use a hoop. Rockinger first coated the fabric with liquid fabric

stiffener and then hung it to dry. She stitched the figures freehand without a hoop while referring to photographs. When the stitching was complete, the fabric stiffener was rinsed out.

Unbacked lightweight fabrics are usually held by a hoop for stitching. A spring-type hoop with a low profile holds this type of fabric better than a traditional hoop equipped with a tightening screw. A

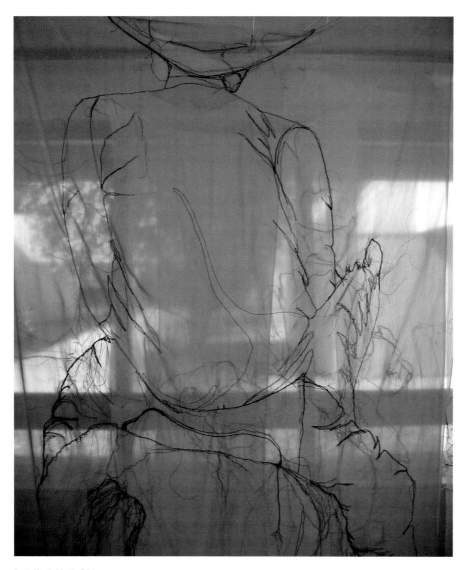

Detail of *Myth Riders*.

hoop is easier to use on a machine that has a platform around the arm. For best results sewing on silk and microfibers, use a 70/10 sharp needle or a Microtex needle, which is thinner and has a slim point.

To maintain the inherent elasticity of knits, stitch in small areas. Back the motifs with a nonwoven stabilizer and trim away the extra after stitching or sandwich the knit between two layers of water-

soluble stabilizer and use a hoop. To prevent damage to knits, use a ballpoint needle. Stitch with a relaxed tension on the fabric in the hoop to keep the motif flat on the fabric, as in the example of spirals on sparkly netting. Stretching the fabric taut in a hoop without a stabilizer will cause interesting bubbles and distortion. If two fabrics are stitched together, particularly if one is translucent, consider cutting away parts of one.

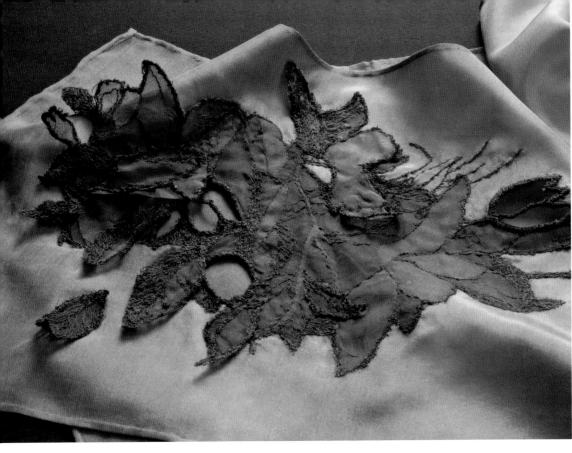

Translucent silk was stitched to lightweight *habutai* (China silk) using a hoop. Be aware that it is easy to lose the soft flexibility of lightweight fabrics with too much stitching.

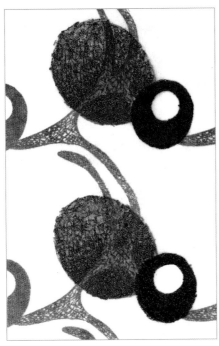

I scanned a drawing into my computer, printed it on heat-transfer paper, and ironed it onto silk organza. Although the translucency remained, the silk became stiff and seemed more like tracing paper. I bonded pieces of gold metallic fabric to the back of the silk, placed the sample in a hoop, and stitched with black and green metallic threads.

For this sample, I chose a loose but smooth plain-weave fabric with a weft of metallic-wrapped thread (shown at the bottom of the photograph). I experimented with a small square of heat-transfer imagery and stitched the outline of a leaf with metallic thread, using a hoop. The fibers moved and crinkled after they were rinsed in water.

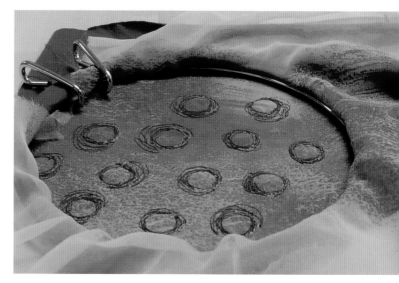

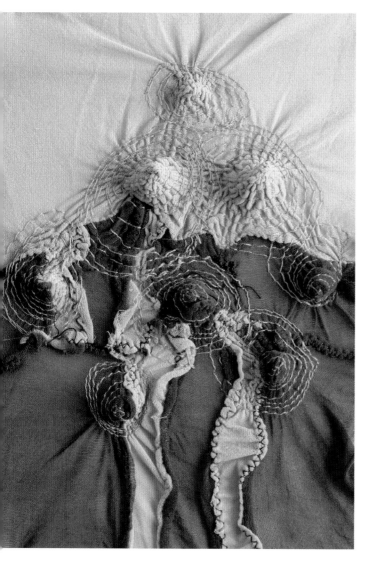

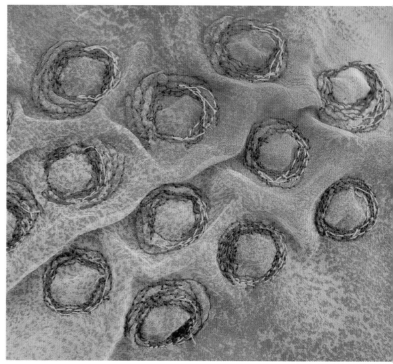

Above Left: Small motifs were stitched on sparkly knitted netting.

Above Right: To exploit the resiliency of lightweight knit fabric, I pulled it taut in a hoop, layered silk chiffon over it, and stitched small circular shapes through both layers.

Below Right: When the knit fabric was released from tension in the hoop, the chiffon bubbled between the stitched areas.

Below Left: In this sample, I stitched concentric circles on nylon-stocking fabric stretched in a hoop. The stitched circles became three-dimensional nipples when the tension was released.

Dissolvable Films and Fabrics

There are many types of dissolvable films and fabrics. Widely available is Solvy, a water-soluble stabilizer produced by Sulky. It comes in several weights, but they all need to be placed in a hoop for stitching. OESD offers a line of "wash-aways," including a very stiff product called Badge Master Aqua Film that requires no hoop (see page 122). Heavier stabilizers are more difficult to rinse away completely, but the stiffness that is left in the stitching can be a bonus in projects where stiffness or three-dimensionality is desired.

Cindy Hickok has tried many types of water-soluble stabilizers. She now uses a lightweight stabilizer, which is what she used for *Very Still Life*, because it rinses out completely. Noriko Narahira used a hot-water-soluble fabric to stitch her *Lace Garment* (see page 120).

Using water-soluble stabilizers allows elements to be positioned in large structures such as Noriko Narahira's *Sounds of Nature* (see page 90). Marian Bijlenga also uses water-soluble stabilizers to create small units of horsehair or fabric and to stitch connections between them as in *Sampler Dots* (see page 107).

For adding elements to a fabric surface, place bits of thread, yarn, or fabric between a water-soluble stabilizer and a base fabric. The stabilizer will prevent the small pieces from catching on the presser foot while stitching. The fabric on which the soluble film is placed can be stretched in a hoop for stitching, or the soluble film can be temporarily attached to the fabric with masking tape (see page 121).

To create lace, sandwich threads, yarns, and fabric bits between two layers of water-soluble stabilizer held in a hoop (see page 123). Unless there is an underlying fabric, stitch over the design lines several times and make sure that the shapes are caught with thread on all sides. When the stitching is complete, rinse out the film. Pin the piece to Styrofoam or a similar foam sheet before rinsing to prevent it from collapsing into an impossible tangle once it is wet. Rinse the sample until it no longer feels sticky and let it dry on the Styrofoam (see page 124).

To inlay a piece of fabric with lace, place the water-soluble stabilizer with completed embroidery over the fabric to which it will be attached. Use satin stitch or a pattern stitch around the lace edge, catching the lace stitching evenly on all sides and stitching through the fabric as well. Trim away the fabric beneath the stitched stabilizer, and trim away any stabilizer that extends beyond the joining satin stitch (see page 125).

Very Still Life, Cindy Hickok 2007, 15½" x 21"
(40 x 54 cm). Thread on water-soluble mesh.
Photographer: Rick Wells. Collection of Jill Wright.

Lace Garment,
Noriko Narahira 1999.
Thread stitched on
hot-water-soluble
fabric. Photographer:
Junichi Kanzaki.
Private collection.

This detail shows the
fabric structure Noriko
Narahira created using
soluble fabric, as well
as her simple but ef-
fective edging.

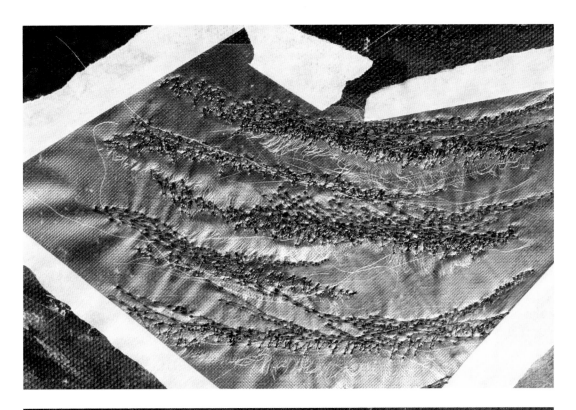

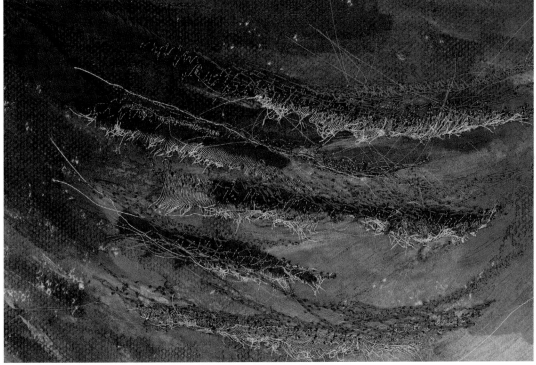

Soluble film can be attached temporarily to fabric
with masking tape, shown here before (top) and after
(bottom) rinsing.

The stitching in this sample was done without a hoop on
Badge Master Aqua Film. This piece has not been rinsed.

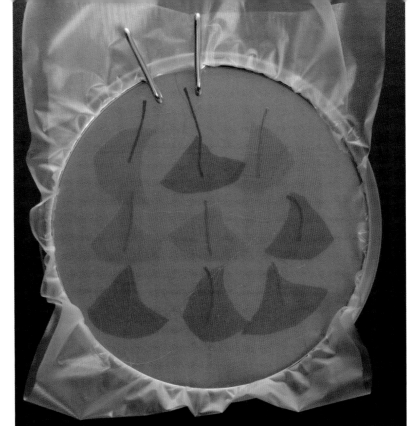

Right: Threads, yarns, and fabric bits can be placed between two layers of water-soluble stabilizer secured in a hoop.

Below: Make your own hoop by cutting a hole in a piece of heavy cardboard of any shape or size and taping the stabilizer sandwich to the bottom side. It will easily slide under the presser foot.

Left: Pin lace to the desired shape on Styrofoam before rinsing.

Below: The completed sample.

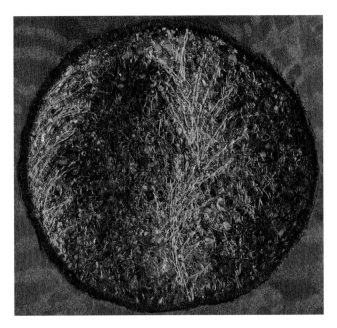

Left: One side of a reversible lace inlay is shown here.

Below: The other side of the same reversible inlay—note the different thread colors.

Opposite: *Variations on "B,"* B. J. Adams 2002, 42" x 42" (107 x 107 cm). Fabric, paint, heat transfer, appliqué, buttons, bows, and stitching. Photographer: PRS Associates. Collection of the artist.

B. J. Adams played with the traditions of trompe l'oeil illusionism by combining realistically embroidered butterflies made with water-soluble stabilizer with heat-transferred images of the embroidered butterflies. For the banana images, Adams drew the changes observed in a single banana every third day, then stitched what she had drawn. She combined heat-transferred images of her drawings with embroidered, appliquéd bananas. The bows and buttons are a combination of real objects and heat-transferred images, and thread was stitched into the holes of both. She embroidered the brushes but added real paint to the bristles. The baseball and words are embroidered.

Below: Detail of *Variations on "B."*

Dyed cheesecloth was embedded and applied to canvas with Golden's Light Molding Paste (a paste with a matte finish designed to build up thickness and texture for acrylic paintings). Paint, fabric bits, and stitching were applied on top.

Painting, Printing, and Stamping Fabrics Before and After Stitching

There are numerous possibilities for using dyes and paints. Jane Dunnewold's book *Complex Cloth: A Comprehensive Guide to Surface Design* (see Recommended Books on page 172) is one of the best. Experiment with ways to integrate stitching with other surface-design techniques.

Left: A black-and-white heat-transfer image was lightly stitched, then white acrylic paint was rubbed into the surface and gently rinsed off so that paint remained in the needle punctures and fabric rather than on the thread. Handstitching was added at the end.

Below: In this sample, hand-dyed fabrics were pieced, stamped, and layered with machine and hand-stitching.

Collaging and Combining Materials and Techniques

You can increase the visual complexity of a piece by incorporating a variety of techniques. This can create a richer experience for viewers, as long as the design and concept remain strong. Technique should never overwhelm content. But, although technique should be integral to the whole, it does not need to be invisible. Seeing the techniques used in the making of a piece allows the viewer to participate visually in the artist's processes.

To experiment with graphite, I started by collaging painted and dyed fabrics that were machine and handstitched in various ways. Next, I painted the sample with a mixture of graphite and gel medium, and then burnished it. I tried sanding the top in the lower right but wasn't happy with the result, so I touched up this area with acrylic paint and added more paint to highlight a few other areas. I finished it with more handstitching.

To see what the full potential for a heat transfer would be, I planned to try one over stitching and fabric ridges (see pages 132 and 133). I knew that the transfer would not show up on a dark ground, so I began by sewing together torn strips of faded pink fabric. I marked off square shapes with masking tape and stitched the squares with an analogous gradation—yellow to blue-green. Then, I applied a heat-transfer image of a typographical map over the stitching because I thought the pattern would be fairly easy to understand and would allow the stitching beneath to show. Although I felt the result was difficult to read, it gave me ideas for future experiments.

A single sample is not enough to explore the full potential of a particular technique or medium. Give yourself time to experiment. You will come up with more good ideas during the process of working than while you're just thinking about the process. Keep asking yourself what other possibilities could be sampled, then try them. For other ideas and examples, see *New Dimensions in Hand and Machine Embroidery* by Jan Beaney and Jean Littlejohn (see Recommended Books on page 172).

Opposite: This sample was designed to experiment with graphite.

In the sample shown at left and below, I wanted to see what would happen to a heat transfer applied over stitching and fabric ridges.

Chapter Five:
Freestyle Machine Embroidery as an Artistic Medium

"Art is about art, and art is about describing the world. But above these functions, art is about exploring what it is to be human."

—Peter London, contemporary teacher, artist, and author

Freestyle machine embroidery and hand embroidery share materials and some processes. While handstitching is slow and considered, with each stitch premeditated, machine stitching is faster and lends itself to rapid stitch sequences. Rather than considering each stitch individually, lines of stitches or blocks of stitches become the units of thought. Although the work methods may be different, the two approaches can work well together.

Both hand and machine embroideries are satisfying to view at close range because the rhythmic textures reflect a process that is relatively direct and familiar. Most people have held a needle and thread at some point in their lives, or have observed someone else sewing. The same can be said of stitches made by a sewing machine. Because people understand what a stitch is, the audience is ready to be engaged. Once viewers understand that they are looking at embroidery, they often seek a viewing distance that is similar to two people in conversation, sometimes even closer, so that they can see and appreciate the fine scale of the stitches. But embroidery is versatile. Its finely scaled textures do not limit the scale of work produced or the range of subjects and approaches.

This chapter contains inspiring work from a few artists who use the sewing machine. Their works are vastly different from each other, but they share an international language made of stitches; they share and appreciate the medium of stitching across cultural and verbal boundaries. Each has a unique vision and each gives us a revelation—that "aha" moment when we see things with a new intensity, experiencing, as Umberto Eco says, "the soul of the things of this world, a materialistic ecstasy."

Landscape Study/Water, Jane Kenyon 2007, 35" x 35" (89 x 89 cm). Thread on water-soluble stabilizer. Photographer: Kenji Nagai. Collection of the artist.

Audrey Walker, Wales

Audrey Walker stitches people who seem at once individual and archetypal. We recognize their glances and the nuances in their expressions. Walker draws upon observations and memories to develop her ideas. She makes drawings during this process, but refrains from resolving an idea with drawing before she begins stitching. She feels it is important to allow the embroidery process to express her intent in ways that are specific to the stitched medium, rather than to reproduce an image that already exists in some other form.

Usually Walker establishes the image with broad areas of machine stitching before developing it further with handstitching. This layer of stitches is thin, allowing the fabric colors beneath to show. In turn, the application of handstitches defines planes and details without obliterating the underlying machine stitches. In this way, each layer contributes to the whole and allows the entire mark-making process to be seen.

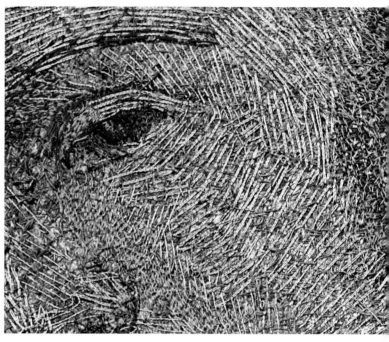

Detail.

Gaze 1, Audrey Walker 1999, 19" × 17" (48 × 43 cm). Pieced fabrics with hand- and machine stitching. Photographer: Phillip Clarke. Private collection.

Detail.

Alice Kettle, England

Alice Kettle combines expressive line and broad areas of color to present archetypal stories of human existence. Building her embroideries with gestures and intuitive marks, she contrasts a sense of human movement and immediacy with surrounding spaces. In describing her work, Kettle says, "The act of making becomes linked with the expression of the story, the threads constitute the words, each one different and able to become something else the moment it joins with another. The narrative evolves through the stitching, a rhythmic adding and taking away, reconstituting and constructing."

Kettle says that stitching opens another dimension into the fabric surface, giving it power through the qualities of different threads, the tensions of the threads, and the processes that pull and distort the fabric. Much of her work is done from the back because many of the threads are too thick to be put through a needle and must by wound onto bobbins. Because she cannot see the finished side as she sews, Kettle must carry the image in her head while working. As she cuts, rejoins, and distorts the surfaces of flexible fabrics, Kettle engages viewers with the play of light as well as with the suggestion of a story that changes with each telling.

Angel, Alice Kettle 2007, 27½" × 19¾" (70 × 50 cm). Machine stitching on fabric. Photographer: Joe Low. Collection of Stephen and Alison Welsh.

Soundings, Barbara Lee Smith 2005, 45" × 120"
(114.5 × 47.3 cm). Painted, collaged, fused, and stitched
synthetic materials. Photographer: Tom Holt.
Collection of Tacoma Community College.

Barbara Lee Smith, U.S.A.

Barbara Lee Smith's rich background in embroidery
informs her current work, which offers panoramic
experiences of place and weather. Although Smith
describes details of places, this body of work is
more about capturing their essences and evoking
the physicality of landscapes. Smith has described
a variety of places, but many suggest the ephem-
eral mists and quiet bodies of water of the Pacific
Northwest. Built of muted and subtle layers, her
pieces present hushed moments and shifting air
currents.

Smith's pieces are constructed with a nonwoven
material similar to Pellon, but which is stiffer
and more translucent. Smith began this piece by
painting large panels of this fabric. More parts and
details of the same material were bonded to the
surface. Her use of map fragments suggests the human desire to assign labels and directions through
place and experience. However, the fragments
are muted and give us the feeling that they are no
longer needed or are memories of a time in the
past. Across the entire surface of each work, Smith
stitches her own topographical map, each as unique
as her fingerprint.

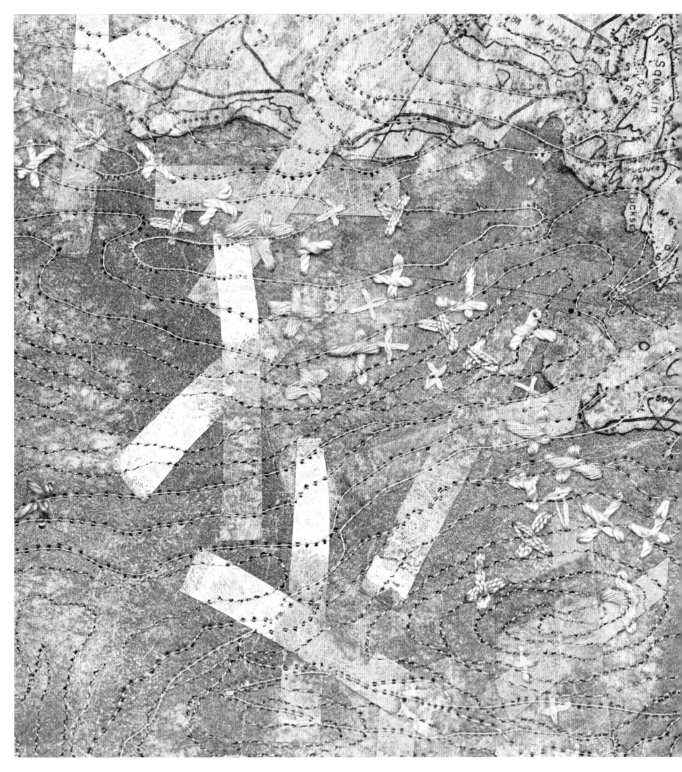

Detail.

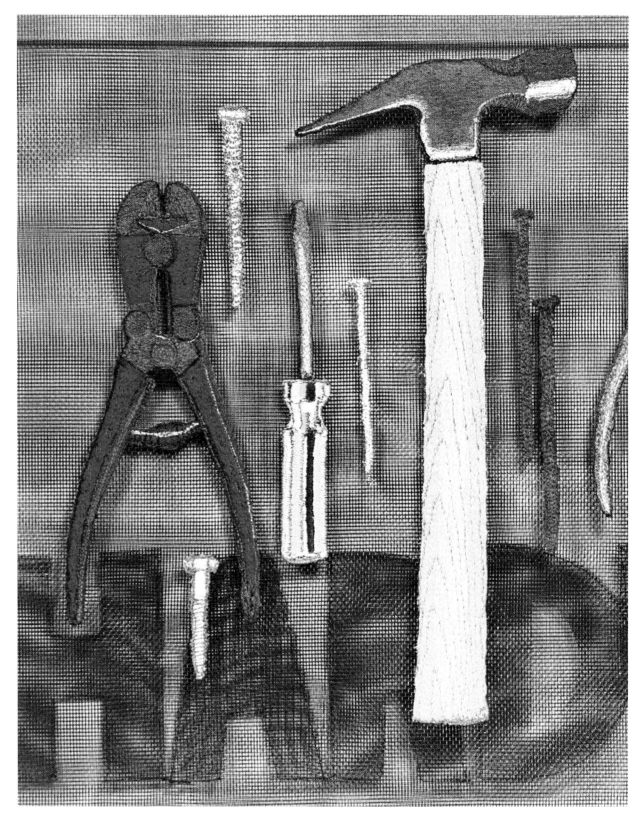

Detail.

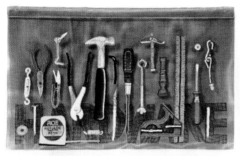

Tireless Tools, B. J. Adams 2005,
15" × 65" (38 × 165 cm). Screening,
thread. Photographer: PRS Associates.
Collection of the artist.

B. J. Adams, U.S.A.

B. J. Adams began her artistic life painting and drawing. After a period of experimental work with fiber arts in the 1970s, she began to focus on fabric and stitching. She enjoys surprising the viewer: some images are surrealistic; others combine realism with real objects. In *Variations on "B"* (see page 126), she combines objects, photographic heat transfers, and realistically embroidered images.

While working on one piece, Adams says that another concept often emerges, and it is this constant, stimulating flow that causes her work to evolve. Her process usually begins with drawings that help her shift from three-dimensional reality to two-dimensional depictions of her source material. She stitches on a water-soluble stabilizer in a hoop, starting with contour drawings that become trompe l'oeil illusions by the time they are taken out of the hoop. These small realistic elements function as both images and objects as they are applied to other surfaces to complete a concept. By taking objects out of one context and placing them in another, she manipulates the connections made by viewers.

Transformed in Silence, Jane Kenyon 2007, 36" × 48" (92 × 122 cm). Thread on water-soluble stabilizer. Photographer: Kenji Nagai. Collection of the artist.

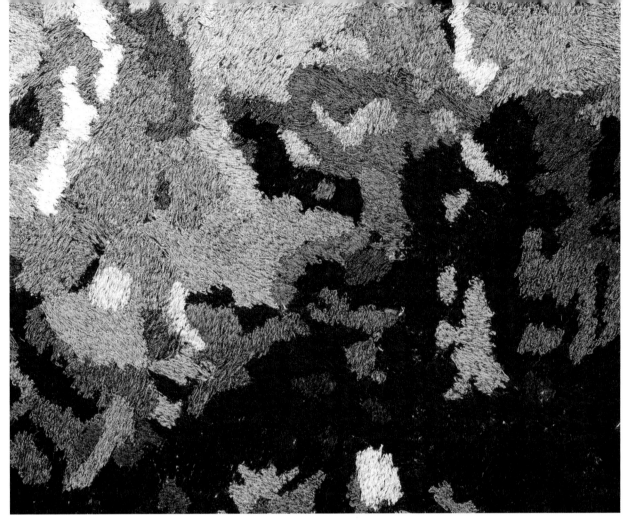

Detail.

Jane Kenyon, Canada

Jane Kenyon's love of surfaces is evident in every one of her pieces. Color is separated into map-like shapes that create elaborate surface patterns. By paying close attention to color values, she is able to exaggerate hue and saturation. She says, "Color is everything in my work, and each artwork is a color study."

For her *Urban Markings* Series (see *Post No Bills* on page 4) she looks at markings left in cityscapes. For this series, she manipulated digital photos of urban surfaces using as many as thirty layers in Photoshop. This allowed her to create images that suggest accretions of peeling paint, graffiti, and decaying posters.

The color separations in *Transformed in Silence* suggest aged surfaces, lichens, and shadows, yet are done with a much wider range of color than is usually associated with rocks. This surprise adds to the interest and wonder of the piece.

Kenyon's large pieces are composed entirely of thread stitched on a water-soluble stabilizer. Threads are blended using more than one color at a time. She stitches in multiple directions to allow the play of light to alter color perceptions and to extend her palette. We are brought close to the subject so that we can experience the full intensity of what it means to observe the physical world.

Succulence, Susan Brandeis 2005, 39" × 79"
(99 × 201 cm). Digitally printed, hand and machine
embroidered, hand beaded, cotton and silk.
Photographer: Susan Brandeis. Collection of the artist.

Susan Brandeis, U.S.A.

Susan Brandeis's passion for making textiles
began with early experiences in sewing, embroidery,
and quilting. She loves many aspects of working with materials, as well as the meditation that
accompanies her processes. Her work embraces
a range of techniques, including dyeing, printing,
piecing, weaving, beading, and stitching. In recent
years, she has been working with digital printing.
Before embracing this new technology, she carefully investigated the pros and cons of the process.
Although it increased the speed of printing and
reduced her exposure to chemicals, it separated her
from the tactile properties of the printing process.
She compensates for this detachment from printing
by adding hand embroidery, machine embroidery,
and beading.

For many years, Brandeis has used nature as her
subject matter. Her work has evolved from general
impressions of nature to more specific places,
plants, and moments. She feels that her sources
of inspiration and her images have become more
intimate and reflective over time.

Detail.

Noriko Narahira, Japan

In Noriko Narahira's huge lace structures and in her more solid forms, she is primarily preoccupied with light and shadow. Her Scene of White series beautifully illustrates how texture can capture light and define form. The forms appear to change throughout the day, reflecting gradual changes in light and shadow.

Narahira has used industrial felt in *Scene of White 2* to make a form that refers to garments. The slashes suggest seams and details of the human body. Holes are like printed polka dots, which change their shape according to how they lie on the three-dimensional form. But these polka dots also penetrate the form to create ever-changing value shifts between the front and the back. This emphasis on layers adds to the depth and volume of the form. Varied densities of zigzag stitching create areas that also shift in value, according to the degree of texture and the amount of light that is absorbed or reflected from the surface.

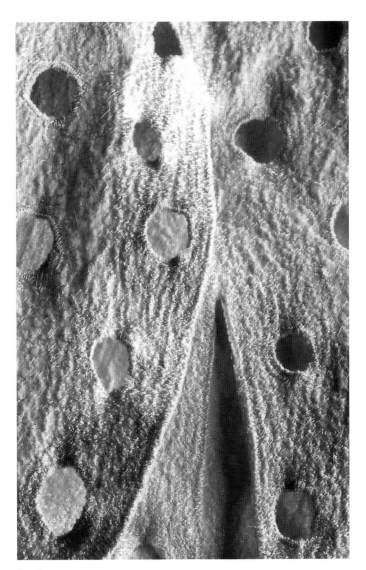

Detail.

Scene of White 2, Noriko Narahira 1999, 59" × 23½" × 31½" (150 × 60 × 80 cm). Industrial felt, thread. Photographer: Junichi Kanzaki.

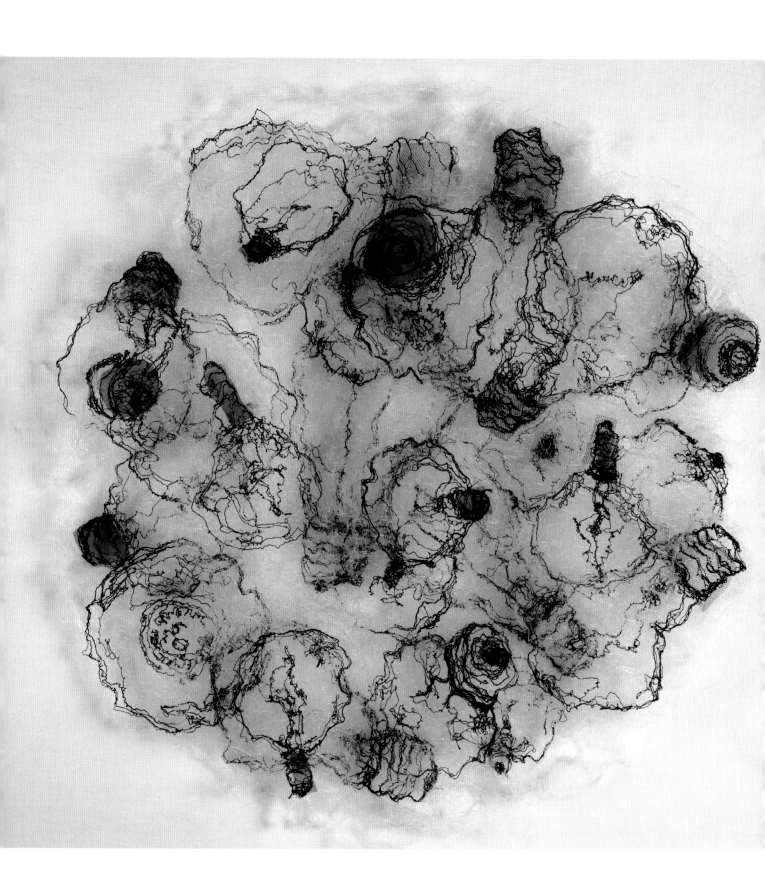

Susanne Gregg, U.S.A.

In this body of work, Susanne Gregg concentrates on transparency and space. She uses clear monofilament thread with a soluble base to create a background on which to stitch delicate line drawings. Once released from the soluble base, the drawings take on a fluidity of their own. The resulting wavy appearance suggests the distortions seen through old glass windowpanes.

Gregg finds the ethereal nature of transparency and space to be alluring. She is able to capture the ambiguity of space often associated with transparency and still keep clarity of image. She says, "A delicate, lacy structure is created where the third dimension is simultaneously real and illusion."

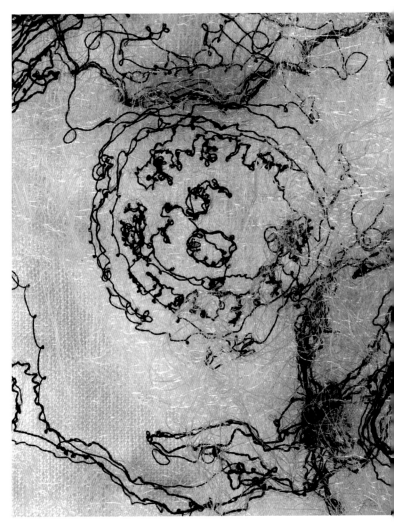

Detail.

Light Bulbs, Susanne Gregg 2008,
24" × 24" (61 × 61 cm).
Monofilament, thread, and bits of
fabric stitched on water-soluble film.
Photographer: John Seyfield.
Collection of the artist.

Sondra Dorn, U.S.A.

Sondra Dorn sees her life as an accumulation of days stacked in layers, eventually becoming one larger whole. The materials and processes she uses in her work become a metaphor for daily living. She says, "Cloth has the ability to absorb and withstand events and maintain its integrity. I layer one action or process on top of another, first embedding the pieces of cloth with information: color, image, texture. I attach layers of cloth with stitched marks and text, creating a physical and metaphorical connection. I then 'burn' or cut away the 'present' to remember the 'past,' changing it irrevocably."

Dorn hand dyes, prints, paints, and draws on her fabrics. She then cuts, reattaches, and collages the pieces together. She uses a combination of hand-sewing, hand embroidery, and freestyle machine embroidery as part of the history of her cloth. Her machine-stitched writing evokes time and the recording of events in letters and diaries and implies unspoken secrets and emotions.

Detail.

Desire: Conceal, Sondra Dorn 2000, 30" × 30" (76 × 76 cm). Collaged fabric with machine stitching. Photographer: Tim Barnwell. Collection of Denise Glick.

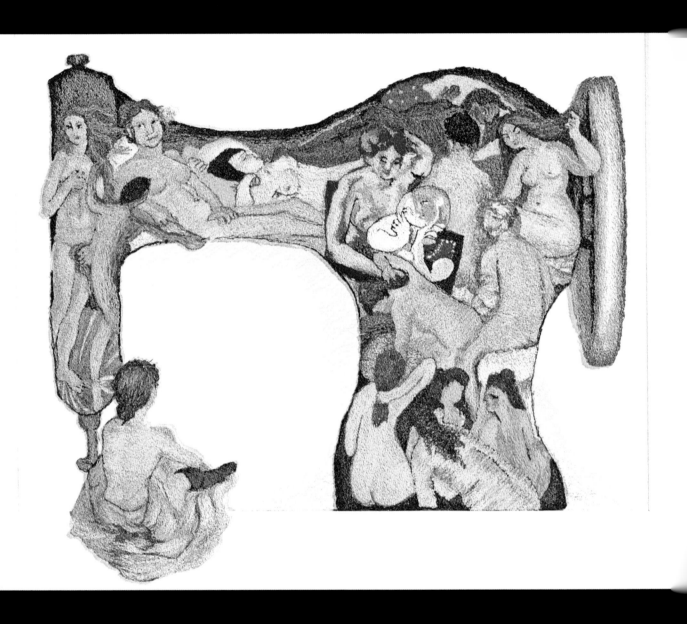

Threadbare: Does Anyone Sew Any More?, Cindy Hickok
2003, 17" × 17" (43 × 43 cm). Thread stitched on
water-soluble mesh. Photographer: Rick Wells.
Private collection.

Cindy Hickok, U.S.A.

When asked about how she gets ideas, Cindy Hickok replies, "Many of my pieces begin because of a title.... Maybe titles are synonymous with ideas for me. Lectures, books, conversations, and, yes, even eavesdropping can provide fodder for my work." She often finds ideas or develops a theme by playing word games.

A few years ago Hickok felt the need to develop her color more and began looking at paintings by "the masters." She decided to emulate their techniques to better understand their use of color and was soon making pieces using characters from the paintings.

Hickok has stitched with rayon threads on water-soluble materials for a number of years, changing products as they improve. By using different bobbin colors, she achieves subtle shading once the stabilizer has been rinsed away. She also mixes colors by layering and juxtaposing thread colors. Visual color mixing is particularly important to Hickok because there are fewer color choices available in rayon threads.

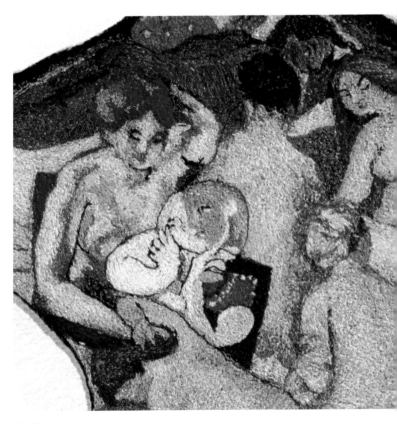

Detail.

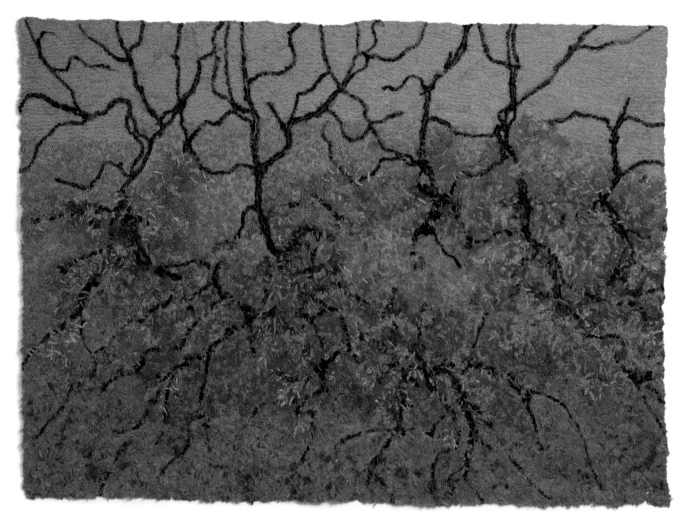

New Life, Jan Beaney 2008, 34½" × 49" (88 × 125 cm).
Hand- and machine stitching on water-soluble film.
Photographer: Michael Wicks. Collection of the artist.

Jan Beaney, England

Jan Beaney stays closely connected to what she observes, recording her observations in sketchbooks for future interpretations in thread. In the work included here, she constructs panels with hand- and machine stitching on soluble film to create new cloth. Without the encumbrance of a fabric structure in the matrix, she finds it easier to penetrate the thread structure with a rich blend of fibers. Her style of combining machine stitching and handstitching melds the materials into a unified surface, while still revealing individual stitches in the finished embroidery.

Although Beaney finds inspiration in fields near her home, she also is influenced by travel. *New Life* was inspired by visits to the Red Centre in Australia. The area had been devastated by fire and new growth created stark contrasts to the color and form of red earth and blackened branches.

Detail.

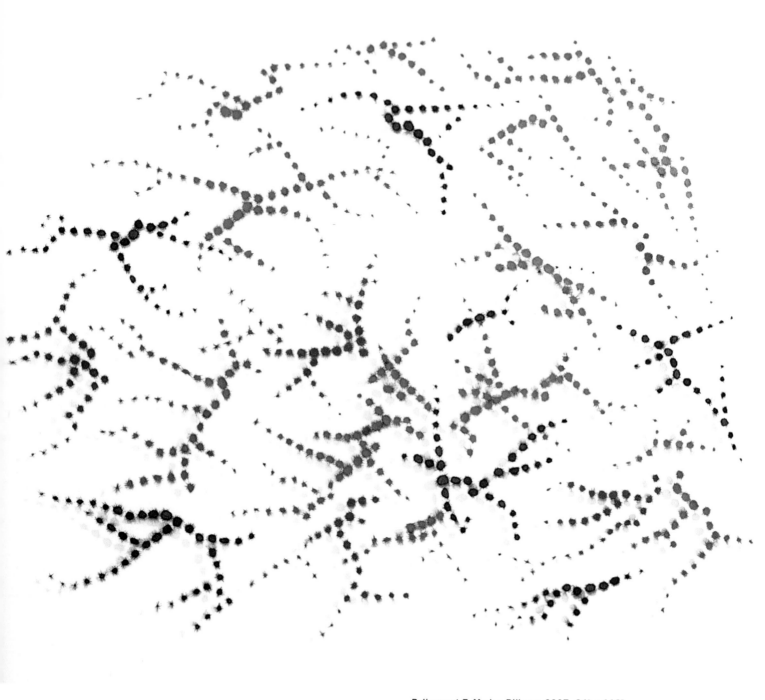

Palimpsest 7, Marian Bijlenga 2007, 84" × 112"
(213 × 284 cm). Horsehair, fabric, monofilament.
Photographer: Ron Zijlstra. Collection of the artist.

Detail.

Marian Bijlenga,
The Netherlands

Marian Bijlenga works in patterns. She is fascinated by the way dots and other small units can connect into lines and larger groups. These groups are organized into patterns, which in turn confine and utilize empty space. Whereas patterns have traditionally been used as surface treatments either to conceal or to accentuate the forms on which they are placed, Bijlenga uses patterns as objects in their own right. She implies a lateral plane, both with the stitched units and with the transparent spaces between the units of her patterns. Additionally, placing the work slightly away from a wall allows her to incorporate the space between the structure and the wall, creating shadow patterns. Bilenga says that instead of drawing on paper, she draws in space using textiles as her materials. She calls her work "spatial drawing."

Bijlenga starts with thread, fabric, horsehair, and materials that are light and flexible. She creates many small, similar forms or units, which are pinned to her studio wall and developed into larger designs and patterns. Once a structure or pattern is developed, the units are connected with transparent thread.

The definition of "palimpsest" is a manuscript that has been reused by scraping off the original text and writing over the top. The result carries traces of past use. In Bijlenga's *Palimpsest* series, she began by mapping the traces of pinholes left on the studio wall of Herman Scholten, a fellow Dutch artist. She transferred these to her own wall as inspiration.

Kay Khan, U.S.A.

Each of Kay Khan's vessels begins with quilting. She uses the layered quilt structure as a sturdy but malleable background on which to build her imagery. The vessels are constructed of many layers of fabric, which are appliquéd as blocks of color. The overlying linear drawings, applied in stitches, supply unifying pattern, detail interest, and structure to the images. The graphic quality of her drawing technique reflects the graphic quality of the text on her forms. Khan works in flat panels and then constructs three-dimensional forms by joining the slabs together with machine stitching.

Each of her forms embodies the concept of containment in two ways. Each piece is a physical container, but the surfaces also become containers for complex networks of thought. Viewers are sometimes drawn to the images, sometimes to the words, and sometimes to the three-dimensional form. Ideas and images are layered so that the human story of each vessel gradually becomes revealed through its components.

Garden of Eden, Kay Khan 2006, 25" × 14" × 6½" (64 × 36 × 17 cm). Cotton, silk, and felt quilted, pieced, appliquéd, and hand- and machine stitched and constructed. Photographer: Wendy McEahern. Courtesy of the Jane Sauer Gallery.

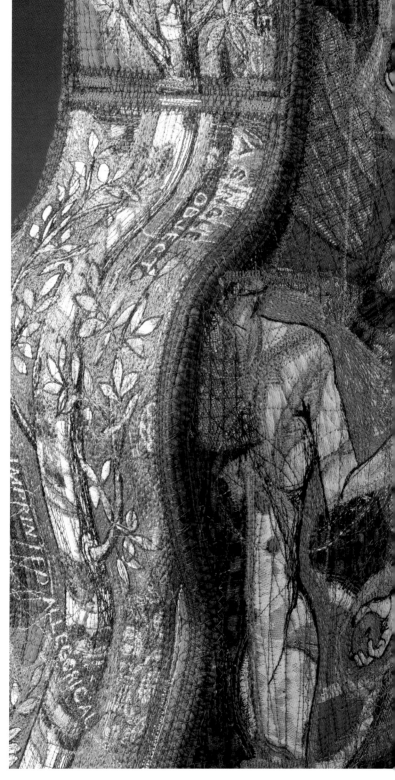

Detail.

Carol's basement studio.

Appendix:
Your Work Space and Equipment

You'll do your best work if you're comfortable and relaxed. When you set up a workspace for machine embroidery, plan for physical comfort. If you hold uncomfortable positions for long hours, your body may retaliate and prevent you from working at all. The right relationship between your chair and your sewing machine will reduce back fatigue. Choose a chair that allows your feet to rest flat on the floor. If your machine has a foot control, the heel of that foot should rest on the floor. Your back should rest comfortably against the back of the chair. Over several hours, a chair with a flat seat may be more comfortable than one with a cupped seat.

Coordinate the height of your sewing-machine table with the height of your chair. If you need to hold your arms out from your body or hunch up your shoulders, the table is too high in relation to the chair. The table is too low if your head and neck have to bend unnaturally over your work. To further reduce neck strain, you can angle the machine so that the back is an inch or more higher than the front. You can purchase a platform to hold a machine at a suitable angle, or you can prop the back with books and magazines and create an angle that is comfortable for you. Your worktable should be very sturdy so that the machine doesn't bounce up and down as you stitch. It's worth the money to get a table big enough to hold lots of thread, as well as your machine and your work. You may want additional side tables or thread racks within easy reach.

Good light is imperative, and the older you get, the more light you need. I work with several light sources

that I can adjust to eliminate shadows from the machine or from my body. Angle the light so it doesn't shine directly into your eyes or bounce off the table and into your eyes. Avoid uneven light that is bright on one spot of your work and weaker elsewhere. For the best color representation, use lightbulbs

Work with your back straight, relaxed, and supported; your shoulders relaxed; your neck relaxed but not bent forward; and your feet resting on the floor.

Do not work with your shoulders hunched, your back curled, or your feet reaching for the floor or foot pedal.

that mimic daylight. These cost more than regular bulbs but can make a big difference in how colors interact. In addition to two windows that provide indirect daylight in my studio, I have an overhead fixture and a smaller fluorescent lamp with a movable neck and head, both with daylight bulbs.

If you wear glasses, you will work more easily if you use single-focus lenses set to the focal point of your work, rather than bifocals or continuous lenses. If your lenses have the wrong focal length, you may find yourself sitting too far back or hunching over your work to see it clearly.

Although sewing machine design constantly evolves, I find that I have little need for many of the new features. In general, the more elaborate the machine, the more that can go wrong. It is crucial to have a strong, high-quality machine that can sew through thick fabric and run for long work sessions. A machine in which the feed dogs can be lowered is preferable to one that comes with a plate to fit over the feed dogs. A zigzag stitch can be useful, but fancy stitches are difficult to integrate successfully into a design. Make sure that both the top-thread tension and the bobbin tension are easily adjustable. It is best if the bobbin casing can be removed easily so that you can adjust the bobbin tension and clean out lint and thread fragments. Whether you buy a new or used machine, be sure to tell the machine dealer what you will be using it for, and always test the techniques and materials you plan to use while you are at the store.

You can machine embroider without any presser foot, but be aware that the stitches will be more difficult to control. You also run the risk of stitching into your fingers because you must hold the fabric very close to the needle. Instead, invest in a darning/embroidery foot that fits your machine. This will allow the fabric to move freely once the feed dogs have been lowered.

Use high-quality bobbins designed specifically for your machine because you will get better results, and they are better for your machine. Generic bobbins don't always fit properly and can cause uneven stitching. Plastic bobbins are particularly bad because they can wear down unevenly and build up static, catching the bobbin so that it doesn't run as smoothly.

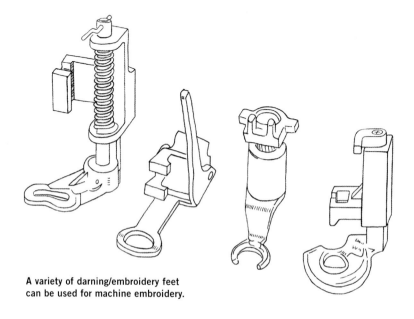

A variety of darning/embroidery feet can be used for machine embroidery.

Basic Color Information

Color is a property of light. When we see color, we see reflected light in different wavelengths. Objects do not have colors as such. They do have the ability to reflect certain wavelengths and absorb others, which creates the sensations of different colors. White objects reflect all wavelengths; black objects absorb all wavelengths. As light changes, so does color.

Colors interact differently when they are used as light (as in the theater) rather than as pigments or dyes that are added to physical material. With the use of light, all colors added together create white light. This is called **additive color**. Think of it this way: the more color you add, the whiter the result. This is the opposite of color as a property of physical objects, pigments, or dyes, where white results when no pigment or colorant is present. This is called **subtractive color**. Think of it this way: the more color you take away or subtract, the whiter the result. Subtractive color is what concerns us as embroiderers, because thread is a physical material.

Subtractive color theory is most often illustrated with a color wheel showing **primary colors** (red, blue, yellow), **secondary colors** (orange, green, violet), and **tertiary colors** (red-violet, red-orange, yellow-orange, yellow-green, blue-green, blue-violet). A more complete picture can be shown on a globe where the traditional color wheel forms the equator. If each hue is represented around the equator and black and white are at the two poles, then the remaining surface of the globe would be covered with all the resulting mixtures—the range of **tints** (mixes with white) and the range of **shades** (mixes

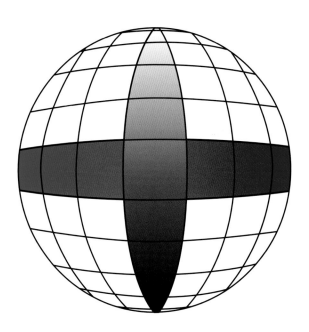

A color globe with the basic color wheel as the equator and mixtures of black and white with those basic colors as longitudinal bands on the globe's surface between pure white and black at the poles.

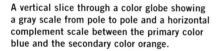

A vertical slice through a color globe showing a gray scale from pole to pole and a horizontal complement scale between the primary color blue and the secondary color orange.

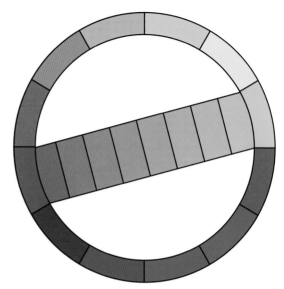

A horizontal slice through a color globe showing the traditional color wheel on the outside and a complement scale across the middle.

with black). Inside the globe there is room for an infinite number of colors, where the basic hues mix with each other and/or with black and white.

Color has three basic properties: hue, value, and intensity. **Hue** (also called chroma) is the name of a color, such as red or green, and also indicates where it is on the equator or color wheel. **Value** refers to how light or dark it is. Some colors in their purest form are light, such as yellow; some are dark, such as violet. Subtractive colors can be darkened or lightened, of course, by adding black or white. When we **raise the value** of a color, making it lighter, we make it reflect more light. Darkening, or **lowering the value**, reduces the amount of reflected light. **Intensity** refers to how pure a hue is. A less intense color would have other colors mixed into it and is considered to be less saturated or more dull. Do not confuse intensity with lightness and darkness.

Local color is what we think of as the actual color of an object. It is the color that is reflected to our eye in normal daylight (for example, the leaves on a tree are green). **Optical color** is the actual color seen by an observer, as opposed to local color, and can be affected by light and atmosphere (trees at sunset may appear orange and trees in the distance may appear blue).

Color may be used representationally or nonrepresentationally, according to the wishes of the artist. Regardless of how true the colors in artwork are to life, they can carry additional impact in ways that are physiological (universal human responses), psychological (personal or subjective responses), and symbolic (cultural responses). Although artists cannot control a viewer's psychological response to their work, they can anticipate symbolic and physiological responses with some predictability.

Studies have shown that each color affects us physiologically in basic ways. Red raises our energy level, sometimes to the point of anger or violence. Blue relaxes or even depresses us, and yellow awakens, cheers, and warms us. Of course, if recognizable imagery is used, that content may outweigh the color response. For example, if the image is a red apple, our response is more likely to reflect our feelings about that particular food rather than a reaction of raised energy or anger.

If one color is more dominant than other colors in an artwork, it can affect the meaning and mood of the piece. This can be achieved three ways: through **color dominance**, **color tonality**, and as an emphasis or **focal point**. When the term **color dominance** is used, one color covers more space in the piece than any other color. When different colors from all parts of the color wheel are used in fairly even proportions, no particular color is likely to affect the mood of the piece. **Color tonality** is the term used when one color is mixed into all the colors of a piece, such as the orange tones that infuse a photograph taken at sunset.

A **focal point** can be created with a color contrast. Contrast clarifies or heightens color by emphasizing differences. There are three basic aspects of color that can contrast: value, hue, and intensity. These aspects of color also can be combined for even greater contrast.

Value Contrast: Each full hue (the point of highest saturation for that color) has a specific location on the value scale. Yellow, being the lightest or highest value, has the greatest contrast with violet, the darkest. Red and green are very close in value. When high-value colors are surrounded by low-value colors or black, they will appear as more pure or as more intense.

Hue Contrast: Colors on opposite sides of the color wheel (or color equator) are called **complements**. When complements are juxtaposed (complementary contrast), they tend to appear as more brilliant or intense.

Our eyes actually see complements that are slightly different from those on the traditional color wheel. While we think of yellow and purple as complements, our brains actually register yellow and ultramarine as complements. Instead of red and green, our brains register magenta and green, or red and a green that is on the blue side. Although the greatest contrast will occur with colors that our brains register as opposites, very effective contrasts can be made with colors that are traditionally opposite on the color wheel. In describing complements, a primary color is often paired with a secondary color, but all the colors on the color wheel have opposites or complements that can be used for contrast.

Hues also can be described as being warm or cool in their relationships to each other on the color wheel. Colors closest to full-intensity yellow are the warmest. Those closest to blue are considered the coldest. Juxtaposing warm and cool colors creates a color temperature contrast.

Intensity Contrast: Contrasts can occur between pure, intense hues and modified or diluted hues. This can be achieved by adding other hues (particularly the complement) to a color, by adding gray, or by adding a combination of both. This type of contrast is often used in representations of depth, with the most intense colors in an artwork used for shapes that appear to be closest to the viewer, and grayer, more modified colors used for distant shapes.

For more information on color, read *Design Basics* (see Recommended Books on page 172).

Three Ways to Reproportion Artwork for Embroidery

When you want to translate a drawing, painting, photograph, or other artwork into an embroidered image, it is sometimes hard to redraw it with the correct proportions, even if it is the same size. I have used three methods to keep the proportions correct when enlarging or reducing an image.

Electronic Method

The simplest method is to scan the image into your computer, then use a program such as Photoshop to enlarge or reduce it as desired. Print the sized electronic image onto heat-transfer paper, then iron it onto fabric. Do not feel that you must slavishly stitch in every detail—edit the information in the transfer as you see fit.

Ratio Method

I used this method for many years while weaving tapestry. It involves easy cross-multiplication. Let's say your original sketch measures 3" × 5" (8 × 13 cm) and you want the longer side of the finished embroidery to measure 14" (36 cm). How long does the short side need to be to maintain the same proportions? The answer is a simple matter of ratios. Make a fraction out of the two known length measurements—14" (36 cm) in the numerator (the top number) and 5" (13 cm) in the denominator (the bottom number). This fraction (ratio) will be in proportion to the shorter side's new and original dimensions and therefore equal to a fraction made

the same way, where the known dimension of the shorter side is the denominator (bottom number). Said another way, put the new measurements for both sides on the tops of the fractions and the original measurements on the bottoms. The unknown new short dimension (called "X" for now) is on top.

$$\frac{14"}{5"} = \frac{X}{3"}$$

Multiply the numerator (top number) of the first ratio by the denominator (lower number) of the second ratio, then multiply the denominator of the first ratio by the numerator of the second ratio. Divide the multiplication of the first cross-multiplication (14" × 3" [36 × 8 cm]) by the denominator of the second ratio (5" [13 cm]). In our example, X = 8.4" (21 cm). Therefore, to maintain the proportions of the original sketch, the 3" (8 cm) side should be enlarged to 8.4" (21 cm).

$$\frac{14" \times 3"}{5"} = X$$

$$\frac{42"}{5"} = X$$

$$8.4" = X$$

To transfer the original image, either draw a grid over it or over a photocopy or an ink-jet copy. To make the grid, divide each side into halves, quarters, eighths, and so on. Divide the larger piece of fabric the same way. Sketch in the shapes on the new grid, using the lines and intersections as guides.

Predetermined Grid Method

This method also begins with a grid drawn over the original or a copy of the original, but in this case, the grid is drawn in predetermined increments, such as 1" (2.5 cm) squares. For example, if you want to enlarge an image fourfold, draw a grid with the same number of squares as on your fabric, but space these lines 4" (10 cm) instead 1" (2.5 cm) apart. Then sketch in the shapes on the new grid, using the lines and intersections as guides.

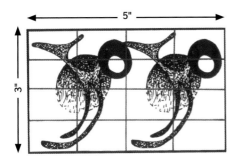

In this example, the original artwork measures 3" x 5" (8 x 13 cm). Draw a grid over the artwork by dividing the piece into halves and quarters in each direction. An enlarged grid measures 8.4" x 14" (21 x 36 cm) and is also divided into halves and quarters in each direction. Here, the new larger drawing has been started using grid intersections and locations within grids for shape placement.

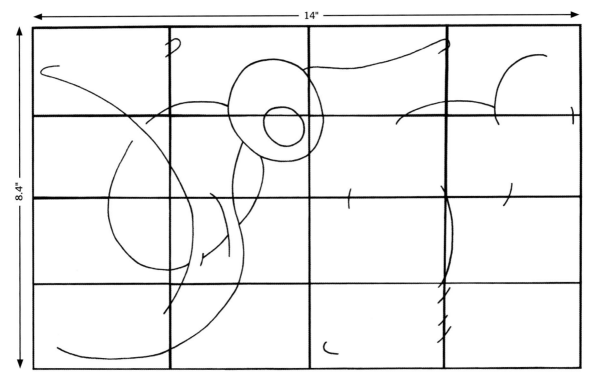

Distortion

If you stitch diagonally (on the bias) on fabric that has been cut with the grain, the fabric will distort diagonally. The heavier the stitching, the more the fabric will distort. Short stitches create less distortion than do long stitches. To a certain extent, you can compensate for the distortion before you start. You may need to make adjustments as you stitch, however, because it is always difficult to predict what the exact degree of distortion will be from stitching.

Begin with a drawing or other artwork that represents how you want your finished piece to look. If the sides are going to be irregular, make your drawing that way. For example, let's say you want an irregularly shaped piece that contains a circle with vertical and horizontal lines.

The fabric will stretch in the direction opposite the stitch direction. This is because you are adding fibers to the matrix of the fabric and the fabric's fibers must move to make way for the addition. Also, the fabric will draw in, or shrink, in the direction of the stitching because the thread pulls together the fibers of the fabric. Draw a distorted grid over your original drawing, slanting the vertical lines of the grid in the same direction as the stretch that you anticipate. Keep the horizontal lines horizontal.

The stretch will be in the opposite direction from the direction that you plan to stitch.

Draw a grid on your fabric that is aligned with the vertical and horizontal grain. Draw this grid to fit the size you have planned for the final piece. Make sure that there is the same number of squares drawn on the fabric as drawn on the distorted grid. If you anticipate using long stitches that will pull in the fabric, you may want to add a little height to each square. Use the grid as a guide for copying shapes and lines in the image. This may seem trickier than it really is because one grid is slanted and the other is not. The new image will slant in the same direction as your planned stitch direction. As you stitch, the piece should gradually shift into the shape you had originally planned.

Fabric before stitching

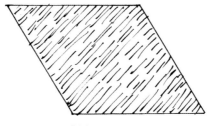

Fabric after stitching

If you stitch diagonally on fabric that has been cut with the grain, the fabric will distort diagonally.

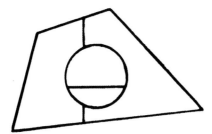

Begin with a sketch of how you want the finished piece to look.

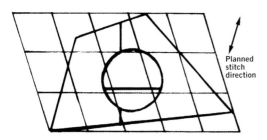

Planned stitch direction

Draw a distorted grid over the drawing, slanting the grid in the same direction you expect the fabric to stretch.

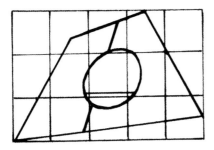

On the fabric, draw a grid that is aligned vertically and horizontally (along the grain of the fabric), then sketch the image on this grid, using the grid lines and intersections as a guide.

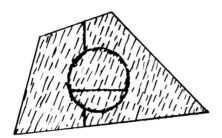

Stitching will cause the fabric to gradually shift into the shape of the original drawing.

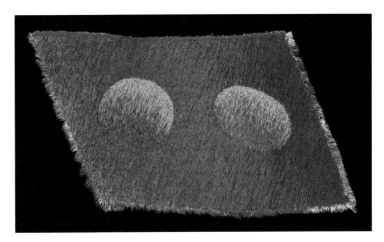

Above: The amount of distortion will depend on your fabric and whether it has been backed with another fabric. This piece began as a rectangle painted with acrylic on unbacked canvas. An oval was painted on the left (with the longest dimension diagonally angled to the right) and a circle on the right. As the fabric distorted with stitching, the oval gradually became a circle and the circle became an oval.

Below: This circle sculpture began as an unpainted circle cut from cotton canvas. Because the stitching radiated from the center in every direction, the fabric stretched outward in multiple directions. Stitching in concentric circles, by contrast, will pull in the fabric and create a bulge or nipple.

Recommended Books

At the time this book was written, the following books were available either through Amazon.com or SoftExpressions.com. Soft Expressions can also be reached by phone at (888) 545-8616.

Bayles, David, and Ted Orland.
Art & Fear: Observations on the Perils (and Rewards) of Artmaking.
Santa Cruz, California: The Image Continuum, 2002.

—*This is a fun and motivational book about letting go of self-doubt.*

Beam, Mary Todd.
Celebrate Your Creative Self.
Cincinnati, Ohio: North Light Books, 2001.

—*This book has lots of ideas and recipes for creating textured surfaces, many of which could be applied to fabric and stitched works.*

Beaney, Jan.
Vanishing Act: Machine Embroidery on Soluble Fabrics. Maidenhead, Berkshire, United Kingdom: Double Trouble Enterprises, 1997.

—*This book is only twenty-four pages, but packed with fabulous, inspiring, close-up photos.*

Beaney, Jan, and Jean Littlejohn.
A Complete Guide to Creative Embroidery. London: BT Batsford, 1997.

—*This book documents the creative process from designing through stitching, and has beautiful illustrations of textures and surfaces using both hand and machine embroidery.*

————. *Gardens and More.* Maidenhead, Berkshire, United Kingdom: Double Trouble Enterprises, 2000.

—*This inspirational book shows what can be done using the garden as a source for machine- and hand-embroidery designs.*

————. *New Dimensions in Hand and Machine Embroidery.* Maidenhead, Berkshire, United Kingdom: Double Trouble Enterprises, 2002.

—*This book covers the combination of machine and handstitching to create wonderful textural surfaces.*

————. *Trees as a Theme.* Maidenhead, Berkshire, United Kingdom: Double Trouble Enterprises, 2001.

—*This book shows how trees are used as a design source.*

Box, Richard.
Flowers for Embroidery: A Step-by-Step Approach.
London: BT Batsford, 2002.

—*This book shows techniques for collaging fabrics with machine and hand embroidery.*

Dunnewold, Jane.
Complex Cloth: A Comprehensive Guide to Surface Design. Bothell, Washington: That Patchwork Place, Inc., 1996.

—*This is a great recipe book for many surface design techniques.*

Finch, Karen, and Greta Putnam.
The Care and Preservation of Textiles.
Berkeley, California: LACIS, 1991.

—*Along with information on making linings for large textiles, this volume contains information on hanging and lighting textiles and other interesting subjects.*

Grey, Maggie.
Raising the Surface with Machine Embroidery. Chicago, Illinois: Quilters' Resource, Inc., 2004.

—*This book contains many ideas on surfaces and textures using machine embroidery with other processes.*

Hedley, Gwen.
Surfaces for Stitch: Plastics, Films and Fabric. Chicago, Illinois: Quilters' Resource, Inc., 2004.

—*This book explores many techniques for collaging and stitching with interesting materials; it has excellent close-up photographs.*

Holmes, Val.
The Encyclopedia of Machine Embroidery. London: BT Batsford. 2003/ Chicago, Illinois: Quilter's Resource, Inc., 2004.

—*This resource provides an alphabetical description of machine-embroidery techniques.*

Lauer, David, and Stephen Pentak.
Design Basics. Fort Worth, Texas: Harcourt Brace College Publishers, 1999.

—*This is a good guide to basic two-dimensional design for artists.*

Littlejohn, Jean.
Voluptuous Velvet. Maidenhead, Berkshire, United Kingdom: Double Trouble Enterprises, 1997.

—*This book has wonderful examples of hand- and machine stitching on velvet, as well as information about printing on and discharging color from velvet.*

Mech, Susan Delaney, MD.
Rx for Quilters: Stitcher-Friendly Advice for Every Body. Lafayette, California: C&T Publishing, 2000.

—*This book has great advice for textile artists, including perspectives on posture, lighting, and avoiding carpal tunnel syndrome.*

Smith, Barbara Lee.
Celebrating the Stitch: Contemporary Embroidery of North America. Newtown, Connecticut: Taunton Press, 1991.

—*This is a guide to North American embroidery with lots of work from many artists, along with their thoughts and insights into their techniques.*

Wong, Wucius.
Principles of Form and Design.
Indianapolis, Indiana: Wiley Publishing, Inc., 1993.

—*This book combines other earlier books into one resource. Foundational design principles are approached from the perspective of their most basic components; it includes great examples for all principles of design.*

Suppliers

Associated Bag Company
400 W. Boden St.
Milwaukee, WI 53207
(800) 926-6100
Fax: (800) 926-4610
associatedbag.com
—*Hospital laundry bags of inexpensive water-soluble material, similar to Solvy, in large sizes; bulk purchases required; listed under "Safety, Medical, and Law Enforcement Supplies/ Safety Medical Bags/Water Soluble." More difficult to rinse out than similar products made for sewing. Also carries bubble wrap and packing supplies.*

Atlanta Thread and Supply
695 Red Oak Rd.
Stockbridge, GA 30281
(800) 847-1001
Fax: (800) 298-0403
store.atlantathread.com
—*Large spools of Gütermann thread and cones of Dual Duty thread.*

Clotilde
PO Box 7500
Big Sandy, TX 75755-7500
(800) 772-2891
Fax: (800) 863-3191
clotilde.com
—*Variety of sewing notions including darning/embroidery feet and water-soluble thread.*

Create for Less
6932 S.W. Macadam Ave., Ste. A
Portland, OR 97219
(866) 333-4463
createforless.com
—*Sewing and craft supplies, including Solvy water-soluble film, machine needles, and threads from Coats and Clark, DMC, and Gütermann.*

Daniel Smith
PO Box 84268
Seattle, WA 98124-5568
(206) 223-9599
(800) 426-6740
Fax: (800) 238-4065
danielsmith.com
—*Art supplies, paint, frames, 10-ounce canvas.*

Dharma Trading Company
654 Irwin St.
PO Box 150916
San Rafael, CA 94915
(800) 542-5227
Fax: (415) 456-8747
dharmatrading.com
—*Fabric, 10-ounce canvas, dye-ready garments, dyes, books, heat-transfer paper.*

Embroidery Online
embroideryonline.com
—*Thread, OESD stabilizers, adhesives.*

Frame Tek
521-D Market St.
Eugene, OR 97402
(800) 227-9934
Fax: (541) 431-4366
frametek.com
—*Various plastic spacers for framing.*

Kreinik
1708 Gihon Rd.
Parkersburg, WV 26102
(800) 537-2166
Fax: (304) 428-4326
kreinik.com
—*Metallic and unusual threads, mini irons.*

Metropolitan Picture Framing
6959 Washington Ave. S.
Minneapolis, MN 55439
(800) 626-3139
Fax: (952) 941-6733
metroframe.com
—*Quality frames and framing supplies.*

Nancy's Notions
333 Beichl Ave.
PO Box 683
Beaver Dam, WI 53916-00683
(800) 833-0690
Fax: (800) 255-8119
nancysnotions.com
—*Extensive range of notions and needles; some Madiera and Sulky threads.*

PRO Chemical & Dye
PO Box 14
Somerset, MA 02726
(800) 228-9393
Fax: (508) 676-3980
prochemical.com
—*Dyes, fabric paint, fabric.*

Red Rock Threads
150 S. Hwy. 160, Ste. 298
Pahrump, NV 89048
(775) 751-9972
Fax: (775) 751-9953
redrockthreads.com
—*Variety of threads, including Presencia and Mettler water-soluble threads.*

Sewphisticted Stitcher
(866) 210-0072
Fax: (866) 210-0072
sewphisticatedstitcher.com
—*Notions plus metallic, rayon, and cotton Madeira threads.*

SewThankful
(Internet only)
PO Box 44124
Rio Rancho, NM 87174
Fax: (505) 896-2888
sewthankful.com
—*Presencia and other threads.*

Testfabrics
415 Delaware Ave.
PO Box 26
West Pittiston, PA 18643
(570) 603-0432
Fax: (570) 603-0433
testfabrics.com
—*Wide range of fabrics prepared for printing and dyeing, including canvas and linen.*

Thai Silks
252 State St.
Los Altos, CA 94022
(800) 722-7455
Fax: (650) 948-3426
thaisilks.com
—*Extensive selection of silk fabrics.*

Index

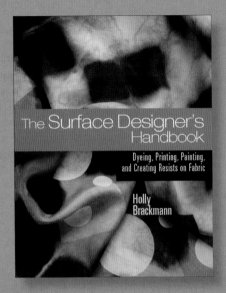
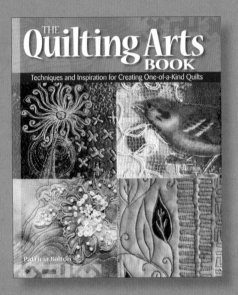